Cambridge Elements ≡

Elements in the Philosophy of Ludwig Wittgenstein
edited by
David G. Stern
University of Iowa

WITTGENSTEIN ON LOGIC AND PHILOSOPHICAL METHOD

Oskari Kuusela
University of East Anglia

CAMBRIDGE
UNIVERSITY PRESS

CAMBRIDGE
UNIVERSITY PRESS

University Printing House, Cambridge CB2 8BS, United Kingdom

One Liberty Plaza, 20th Floor, New York, NY 10006, USA

477 Williamstown Road, Port Melbourne, VIC 3207, Australia

314–321, 3rd Floor, Plot 3, Splendor Forum, Jasola District Centre,
New Delhi – 110025, India

103 Penang Road, #05–06/07, Visioncrest Commercial, Singapore 238467

Cambridge University Press is part of the University of Cambridge.

It furthers the University's mission by disseminating knowledge in the pursuit of
education, learning, and research at the highest international levels of excellence.

www.cambridge.org
Information on this title: www.cambridge.org/9781108986649
DOI: 10.1017/9781108981125

© Oskari Kuusela 2022

First published 2022

A catalogue record for this publication is available from the British Library.

ISBN 978-1-108-98664-9 Paperback
ISSN 2632-7112 (online)
ISSN 2632-7104 (print)

Wittgenstein on Logic and Philosophical Method

Elements in the Philosophy of Ludwig Wittgenstein

DOI: 10.1017/9781108981125
First published online: May 2022

Oskari Kuusela
University of East Anglia

Author for correspondence: Oskari Kuusela, o.kuusela@uea.ac.uk

Abstract: This Element outlines Wittgenstein's early and later philosophies of logic, and explains Wittgenstein's views regarding the methodological significance of logic for philosophy. Wittgenstein's early philosophy of logic is presented as a further development of Frege's and Russell's accounts of logic, and Wittgenstein's later philosophy as a response to problems with his early views, including confusions about idealization and abstraction in logic. The later Wittgenstein's novel logical methods, such as the method of language-games, are outlined, and the new kind of logical naturalism developed in his later philosophy described. I conclude by discussing the later Wittgenstein on names.

Keywords: Wittgenstein, logic, philosophy of language, philosophical method, models

ISBNs: 9781108986649 (PB), 9781108981125 (OC)
ISSNs: 2632-7112 (online), 2632-7104 (print)

Contents

Introduction

This Element provides an introductory overview of Wittgenstein's philosophy of logic and his view of the contribution of logic to philosophy and its methodology. I start with the early Wittgenstein's modification of Frege's and Russell's philosophies of logic. Importantly, although Wittgenstein's early philosophy of logic is of interest in its own right, it also constitutes the background for his later philosophy of logic and methodology to which most of this Element is dedicated. As Wittgenstein explains in the preface to the *Philosophical Investigations*, his later work is, to a significant extent, a response to the 'grave mistakes' of his early philosophy. Nevertheless, he also maintains that his early philosophy constitutes the background against which his later thought can 'be seen in the right light'. This can be understood in the sense that in his later work Wittgenstein seeks to do both, to reconceive and to correct his early philosophy of logic as well as to further develop some of its key insights, for example the point that logical necessity can't be expressed in terms of true/false propositions or theses, and that logic therefore can't be clarified in such terms. In what follows, besides contrasting Wittgenstein's philosophy of logic with those of Frege and Russell, I note certain similarities and differences between Wittgenstein and the views of other analytic philosophers who have likewise sought to develop this approach through considerations relating to methodology and philosophy of logic, namely Rudolf Carnap, W. V. Quine, and Saul Kripke. This provides a context to Wittgenstein's philosophy of logic and philosophical methodology which, I hope, helps to assess his contributions to philosophy in relation to contemporary analytic philosophy.

To start from his early work, in his *Tractatus Logico-Philosophicus* Wittgenstein sought to introduce a logical methodology for dealing with philosophical problems, writing in the preface that the book 'shows ... that the way these questions are posed rests on a misunderstanding of the logic of our language'. Moreover, he states that 'I'm of the opinion that the problems have in essentials been finally solved' and that 'the *truth* of the thoughts communicated here seems to me unassailable and definitive'. This raises the question, what problems did Wittgenstein have in mind? In a letter to Russell he says that he has written a book where 'I believe I've solved our problems finally', indicating that he means the problems relating to logic he had been working on with Russell (CL: 111).[1] Later in the summer of that year, however, he tells

---

[1] The preface is dated to 1918, whilst this letter is from March 1919.

    I have often amended translations from Wittgenstein's works, sometimes using both the Ogden and Pears-McGuinness translations as the basis of quotations from the *Tractatus*. When no published translation exists for quotations from Wittgenstein's *Nachlass*, the translation is mine.

Russell in response to his queries that Russell has failed to understand his book's 'main contention' pertaining 'to the cardinal problem of philosophy', which concerns the question of what can be said in language and what can only be shown by language (CL: 125). Thus, it isn't clear to what extent Russell and Wittgenstein ultimately shared an understanding of relevant problems, even though 'our problems' certainly must have to do with their collaboration on logic. Relatedly, Wittgenstein describes his concerns in his pre-Tractarian *Notebooks* by saying that his '*whole* task' consists in 'explaining the nature of proposition', which, however, also means explaining the 'nature of all being' (NB: 39). At another point he describes his concern with the 'foundations of logic' as having extended to cover 'the nature of the world' (NB: 79). And indeed, for the early Wittgenstein these questions about the nature of propositions, foundations of logic, and the nature of the world or being did constitute different aspects of a single question.[2]

More specifically, the central question of logic, as understood by Frege and Russell, and Wittgenstein following them, was to determine the principles that govern thinking that aims at a truth. Accordingly, the notion of a proposition (Russell) or a thought (Frege) as something capable of being true/false occupies a central place in Frege's and Russell's logical systems, constituting the core notion of their logical languages. Following them, the early Wittgenstein likewise sought to explain the logical principles governing true/false thought or language use by clarifying what he called 'the general propositional form' or 'the essence of proposition'. Thus he aimed to account for the principles governing thinking that aims at truth in terms of one single core notion, motivated by the idea that logic constitutes the standard of simplicity and clarity. This would then also provide an account of the essence of the world or all being, insofar as they constitute objects of thought (TLP 4.5, 5.45–5.4541, 5.47–5.471).

But whilst the preceding is already an ambitious set of problems to solve, Wittgenstein's aspirations may have been even more far-reaching. Following Russell in regarding all genuinely philosophical problems as logical, he seems to have thought that the logical method of the *Tractatus* would contain the key to the solution of not just the problems he was directly addressing but all philosophical problems. Thus understood, in claiming that 'the problems' have been solved 'in essentials' he's saying that the logical methodology introduced in the book makes it possible to solve any philosophical problem whatsoever, including problems not discussed in the book. This brings to view the programmatic character of Wittgenstein's book, criticized by him later. And indeed, perhaps

---

[2] This point has been emphasized by Marie McGinn 2006.

genuinely believing that he had managed to spell out *the* method that could be used to solve all philosophical problems, Wittgenstein left philosophy. By the time he returned about ten years later, however, he had realized or came to realize that his early account of logic covered only part of the functioning of language/thought. It was not complete in the sense of accounting for all the logical principles governing thinking that aims at truth. Consequently, although the *Tractatus'* logical methodology might be helpful in tackling some philosophical problems, it couldn't be assumed to contain the key to the solution of them all.

In the *Philosophical Investigations*, in the work leading to it from the early to mid 1930s, and thereafter, Wittgenstein sees matters differently, although he holds on to the conception that all philosophical problems are logical. 'Merely recognizing the philosophical problem as a logical one is progress. The proper attitude and the method accompany it' (LW I, §256/MS 137: 104b).[3] Mentioning the concepts logic and sentence or proposition (*Satz*) in the preface among the six key themes of the book (in addition to meaning, understanding, foundations of mathematics, and states of consciousness), he had meanwhile realized that 'Language is much more complicated than the logicians and the author of *Tractatus* have imagined' (MS 152: 47; cf. PI §23, RPP I §920). Partly the 'grave mistakes' in his earlier book then relate to this – but also to more general assumptions about logic and philosophy that got him trapped in this simplistic conception of language. Accordingly, an important issue Wittgenstein addresses in his later philosophy is the problem of dogmatism, relating to how the assumptions of philosophical theorizing lead philosophers to false simplification, and how it's possible to simplify and idealize in philosophy without falsifying.

It's controversial whether the later Wittgenstein 1) rejects or 2) 'merely' radically rethinks and further develops the *Tractatus'* approach that involves regarding language as a calculus. On the first interpretation Wittgenstein rejects the conception of language as a calculus and the view that the uses of language can be clarified by means of calculus-based logical methods. As Peter Hacker, a leading representative of the first approach, explains, Wittgenstein's later philosophy of language 'repudiates conceptions of language as a calculus of definite rules on the model of the predicate calculus' (Hacker 1996: 128). 'In place of the conception of language as a calculus of rules, we are offered a conception of a language as a motley of language-games' (Hacker 1996: 125). This implies

---

[3] This remark (from 1948) is made in connection with a discussion of the problem of whether all behaviour could be dissimulation, but I believe it generalizes. In his *Nachlass* Wittgenstein often stops to make general remarks on philosophy and its methods in the midst of dealing with specific problems.

a radical break between Wittgenstein's early and later philosophy. Rather than developing his early approach by introducing new methods and correcting the errors of his early philosophy of logic, the later Wittgenstein replaces his early account of language with a different one. Corresponding to this, he substitutes for his early logical method an approach to philosophy as a grammatical investigation that clarifies the rules according to which language is used. Whilst language on this account 'is indeed rule-governed', it's not governed by strict and definite rules like a calculus, but only in the 'more or less loose manner in which games are rule-governed' (Hacker 1996: 125).

On the second interpretation the later Wittgenstein's primary objection is to his early view that there could be something like *the* logical method, a definite logical methodology universally applicable in all areas of thought and language use that could be used to clarify all sensible forms of language use, and to solve all philosophical problems. As he emphasizes:

> In philosophy it is not enough to learn in every case *what* is to be said about a subject, but also *how* one must speak about it. We always have to begin by learning the method of tackling it.
>
> Or again: In any serious question uncertainty extends to the very roots of the problem.
>
> One must always be prepared to learn something totally new.
>
> Among the colours: kinship and contrast. (And that is logic.) (RC §§43–46/MS 173: 11v–12v; cf. PI §133)

On the second interpretation Wittgenstein continues to regard calculus-based logical methods as a special case of logical methodology. Rather than rejecting and replacing the *Tractatus'* account of language with a different one, he recognizes that different logical or philosophical methods involve different conceptions of language, none of which can be adopted as *the* true one that excludes all others similarly to a true philosophical thesis. As this indicates, the controversy extends to the question of whether Wittgenstein's later approach implies a commitment to some particular account of language, comparable to the *Tractatus'* commitment to the view of language as a calculus. Although this Element doesn't aim to solve this interpretational dispute, I will outline reasons to think that Wittgenstein's later philosophy is best understood as radically rethinking the *Tractatus'* approach (see Section 2). Regardless of which interpretation might get Wittgenstein right on this point, if either, both nevertheless agree that Wittgenstein continues to think of philosophical problems as involving logical-linguistic unclarities, and that their solution requires clarification of relevant linguistic locutions. The dispute concerns specifically the relation between logic in the early Wittgenstein and his later grammatical investigations.

Following the discussion of Wittgenstein's early philosophy in Section 1, and his criticisms of his early approach in Section 2, Section 3 describes the novel logical methods introduced by the later Wittgenstein, and the new kind of philosophical/logical naturalism developed in his later work. In order to illustrate the complexity of language and to connect Wittgenstein with certain more recent discussions in logic and philosophy thereof, Section 4 outlines Wittgenstein's views on different kinds of names in relation to Russell, John Searle, and Kripke.

1 Early Wittgenstein's Reconfiguration of Frege's and Russell's Logic

As Wittgenstein acknowledges in the Preface to the *Tractatus*, the greatest stimulus for his thought came from Frege and Russell. This has to do with their development of logical methods to be used for logical analysis and for addressing philosophical problems, and with questions about the foundations of logic to which the development of such methods gives rise. Here the notion of a logical language (symbolism or notation) of the kind that Frege and Russell had developed independently of one another plays a crucial role.[4] Inspired by G. W. Leibniz's idea of a universal language, characteristic of a Fregean–Russellian logical language is that it would enable one to bypass the vagueness and ambiguities of natural language so as to express conceptual content precisely, and that in it inferences would be governed by strict logical rules that prevent fallacies, unlike the rules of natural language (Frege 1882–3/1972b, 1882/1972c). A language of this kind could then be deployed as an instrument for the logical analysis of judgements and concepts, thus providing us with 'a perspicuous presentation of the forms of thought' (Frege 1882/1972c: 89). Or, as Russell emphasizes, it would help to see beyond merely linguistic distinctions to which nothing corresponds in reality, and 'show at a glance the logical structure of the facts asserted or denied' (Russell 1918/2010: 25).

The significance of such a logical language is indicated by Frege's originally coming to develop his concept-script (*Begriffsschrift*) for the purpose of clarifying the notion of a number as part of his attempt to establish a foundation for arithmetic, whereby he was forced to realize the unsuitability of natural language for the task due to its imprecision (Frege 1879/1972a: 104). However, Frege was fully aware of the general importance of such a logical language for philosophy, that is, how it enables one to keep track of inferences and their presuppositions, so that presuppositions won't slip in unnoticed, creating gaps in inferences (1882/

---

[4] Naturally, they drew on work of earlier mathematicians and logicians. For the history of relevant developments, see Grattan-Guinness 2000.

1972c: 89). Russell went even further in his optimism about the new logical methods, asserting that the 'new logic' would make progress possible in philosophy comparable to the progress made in physics after Galileo's introduction of mathematical methods (Russell 1914/1926: 68–69, 243). Further, Russell maintained that any properly philosophical problems could now be recognized as logical, and that with the help of the new logical methods they could be solved through a piecemeal collaborative investigation in a way that 'must command the assent of all who are competent to form an opinion' (Russell 1914/1926: 69; cf. 43). Thus, it seemed that philosophy could at last embark on a path of progress similar to the sciences, instead of being an idiosyncratic enterprise where there are as many views as there are philosophers.

Wittgenstein accepted Frege's and Russell's views about the significance of a logical language, and gave it an even more important place as the proper way to articulate an account of logic, instead of logical theses. In the process he exposed certain tensions in Frege's and Russell's views with the purpose of developing their ideas further, eventually turning some of their ideas back against them and the philosophical tradition more generally. Significantly, Wittgenstein also followed Russell on the point that philosophical problems are logical. Insofar as they have a solution, this must therefore be sought by means of a logical investigation. However, Wittgenstein was also convinced that the way in which philosophical problems have been traditionally posed involved fundamental logical confusions.

> Most propositions and questions that have been written about philosophical matters are not false, but nonsensical. We cannot, therefore, give any answers to questions of this kind, but only establish their nonsensicality. Most questions and propositions of philosophers result from a failure to understand the logic of our language. . . .
>
> And so it is not surprising that the deepest problems are really *not* problems. (TLP 4.003)

The right response to philosophical problems would therefore not be trying to answer the questions in the terms in which they are expressed. It's to logically examine the questions and statements of philosophers with a view to clarifying logical unclarities or confusions underlying them. Accordingly, Wittgenstein writes: 'The correct method of philosophy would be this: To say nothing except what can be said . . . and then always when someone wished to say something metaphysical, to demonstrate that he had given no meaning to certain signs in his propositions' (TLP 6.53).[5] Thus, philosophy is to be understood as an

---

[5] This is not the method practised in the *Tractatus* which, as I will explain, employs nonsense to introduce a methodological framework for logical analysis. Logical analysis then allows one to

activity whose aim is not the articulation of theories or doctrines but 'the logical clarification of thoughts', whereby the result is not 'philosophical propositions' but 'propositions becoming clear' (TLP 4.112). Through such clarifications philosophy then aims to 'demarcate the thinkable from within through the thinkable' or the 'unsayable by clearly laying out the sayable' (TLP 4.114, 4.115; cf. 4.112–4.116). However, it's important not to assume that the term 'metaphysical' in 6.53 is used in a pejorative sense, more or less synonymous with bad philosophy, as it was used by the logical positivists inspired by Wittgenstein (see Carnap 1931/1959).[6] Rather, Wittgenstein seems to use 'metaphysical' in a specific sense, with metaphysics involving a specific kind of confusion connected with attempts to articulate true propositions or theses about universal, exceptionless, non-empirical necessities pertaining to the essence of things; that is, to assert necessary truths such as metaphysicians have aspired to do. (He continues to criticize this approach in his later philosophy; Z §458/RPP I §949.)

As Wittgenstein sees it, there's a 'confusion, very widespread among philosophers, between internal and proper (external) relations', an internal property being one in the case of which it's 'unthinkable that its object doesn't possess it', and likewise for internal relations (TLP 4.122–4.123). Corresponding to this, the confusion about how philosophical problems are posed, spoken of in the *Tractatus*, can be understood as having to do with attempts to articulate theses about necessary or essential properties or relations that are constitutive of the identity or essence of relevant objects or states of affairs. If Wittgenstein is right, it isn't possible to speak of such essential necessities in terms of true propositions or theses, contrary to what metaphysicians have assumed. Instead, a different approach must be adopted that takes its lead from the following: 'The existence of an internal property of a possible state of affairs is not expressed by a proposition, but it expresses itself in the proposition which presents that state of affairs, by an internal property of this proposition' (TLP 4.124); 'The existence of an internal relation between possible states of affairs expresses itself in language by an internal relation between the propositions presenting them' (TLP 4.125). It's in connection with this issue of the expressibility of what is necessary or essential that the Fregean–Russellian logical language acquires new philosophical significance for Wittgenstein, and he

---

practise philosophy purely formally, without putting forward any substantial propositions about reality, only focusing on the clarification of what is said, as described in 6.53. In laying out the method for logical analysis, the *Tractatus* can be described as concerned with the foundations of logic, clarifying its nature and central notions.

[6] Early on, logical positivism significantly affected the interpretation of Wittgenstein's philosophy, whilst in private correspondence in the early 1930s Wittgenstein expressed the wish not to be associated with it as a school (see Kuusela 2019c: 258–9).

moves beyond the philosophical positions and philosophies of logic of Frege and Russell, as I will explain. An important question now arises about the right way to express essential logical or philosophical necessity, a question which Frege and Russell weren't particularly concerned with beyond their rejection of psychologistic accounts of logic. (Psychologism portrays the principles of logic, not merely the capacity of humans to grasp them, as dependent on human psychology, thus regarding the principles of logic as empirical principles of psychology.)

The confusion underlying philosophical questions and propositions with which Wittgenstein is occupied can thus be connected with what he described to Russell as the cardinal problem of philosophy and the main contention of his book, that is, what it's possible to say in language versus what language, in Wittgenstein's terminology, can only show (CL: 125; cf. introduction). The widespread confusion about internal properties and the problem about how philosophical problems are posed can therefore be identified as partly motivating Wittgenstein's philosophy of logic. (It seems fair to describe the problem of whether it's possible to articulate truths or true theses about essential non-empirical necessities as the cardinal problem of philosophy, since this is just what metaphysicians have tried to do, mostly taking this possibility for granted, with Hume and Kant as important exceptions.)

1.1 Wittgenstein's Rejection of the View of Logic as a Science and of Logical Theses

So why does Wittgenstein think it's not possible to express that which is necessary and essential, as opposed to merely contingent, in terms of true/false propositions or theses? Why can't there be true propositions/theses about logic, and how can logic be clarified, if not by means of propositions/theses? The first step towards explaining this can be taken by outlining Wittgenstein's reasons for rejecting Frege's and Russell's accounts of logic as a science that establishes substantial truths about logic, including the principles governing correct inference, and which, on this basis, prescribes how we ought to think and infer.[7]

Wittgenstein's basic point is simple. In order for thinkers and language users to be able to think or speak, including inferring and judging the correctness of inferences, they must already know – tacitly, if not explicitly – the logical principles governing thought and language. Otherwise they couldn't think or

---

[7] Whilst the interpretive tradition has usually explained Wittgenstein's rejection of theses or theories as a consequence of his own theory of language, the so-called picture theory of language, this is, arguably, to put the cart before the horse (see Kuusela 2021 and forthcoming). I return to this in Section 1.4.

use language to begin with, it being part of the linguistic capacity of speakers that they can tell, with certain fallible reliability, properly formed propositions from nonsensical strings of signs, and that they, for example, understand that nothing follows from mere gibberish. Indeed, given the short history of logic in comparison to the history of humanity, it seems clear that people had been making inferences and judging their correctness long before logicians came around, and began systematizing the principles governing inferences. Nor could logicians have taught people how to infer correctly. In the absence of a capacity to use language no one would have understood their instructions and principles.

The principles of logic, therefore, must be assumed to be already known to thinkers and language users by virtue of their being thinkers/language users.[8] But if so, logic can't be like the sciences that establish truths about their objects of investigation and then inform others about their discoveries. Although it makes perfect sense to inform someone about the discovery of truths or facts – for example, whether there's life on Mars – no one can be informed about what they already know. Interestingly, Wittgenstein's view of logic as already known to thinkers and speakers is foreshadowed in Russell's lectures in 1914, where he says that those capable of understanding discourse must already possess a tacit comprehension of logical forms – which means that they must already have a comprehension of the principles governing inference, since logical inference according to Russell depends on logical form (Russell 1914/1926: 53). But it was left to Wittgenstein to expose this tension in Russell's philosophy of logic. For it can't be that both a) thinkers/speakers already know the principles of logic, and b) logic is a science that informs thinkers/speakers about those principles, establishing on this basis prescriptions that they must respect in order to think/speak logically. Accordingly, Wittgenstein criticizes Russell's theory of types for its aim of establishing such prescriptions (TLP 3.331–3.333; CL: 125). Likewise, *pace* Frege, logic can't be understood as a 'normative science' that prescribes how one must think in order to reach the truth (Frege 1897/1979: 128).

Instead, the task of logic is to clarify to thinkers and language users the principles of logic that they already know; logic articulates clearly and by so doing explicates relevant principles that thinkers/speakers already tacitly know. Rather than a prescriptive science, logic is thus a clarificatory discipline. Wittgenstein explains the key point in terms of a principle regarding the status of logic: 'Logic takes care of itself; all we have to do is to look and see how it

---

[8] It's part of the notion of being a thinker or a language user that they can think and use language. Insofar as this capacity involves a comprehension of logic, as both Wittgenstein and Russell maintain, comprehension of logic can be regarded as part of the capacity to think and use language. As noted, however, this doesn't mean that thinkers/speakers can articulate those principles or have an explicit knowledge of them.

does it' (NB: 11/MS 101: 39r), a point which he described as 'an extremely important and profound insight', when first noting it down in 1914 (NB: 2/MS 101: 13r). Accordingly, the principle that logic looks after itself or takes care of itself constitutes a crucial part of the *Tractatus*' philosophy of logic. Logic takes care of itself in that it doesn't need to be upheld or guarded by the prescriptions of logicians. What counts as a correct inference and what it makes sense to say doesn't depend on logicians, but on thought and language themselves, and on how, corresponding to this, we use our signs to express ourselves. As the *Tractatus* explains:

> Logic must take care of itself.
>
> If a sign is *possible*, it must also be able to signify. Whatever is possible in logic is also permitted. ('Socrates is identical' means nothing because there is no property called 'identical'. The proposition is nonsense because we have failed to make an arbitrary determination, not because the symbol, in itself, would be illegitimate.)
>
> In a certain sense we cannot make mistakes in logic. (TLP 5.473, cf. 5.4733)

That we can't make mistakes in logic 'in a certain sense' doesn't mean that we are infallible about it. In that case there would be nothing to clarify, no room for logic and philosophy as clarificatory activities. Wittgenstein's remarks on the logical confusions of philosophers make clear that this isn't what he thinks. When such logical unclarities or confusions arise, we must clarify the workings of thought and language, and how linguistic signs have been used in trying to express thoughts or propositions. Crucially, however, our mistakes are confusions about what we already know. Logical clarifications constitute reminders about what we already know, not prescriptions.[9]

The preceding doesn't yet exhaust the significance of Wittgenstein's principle that logic looks after itself. This insight also makes unnecessary any appeal to self-evident truths in logic, contrary to Frege and Russell. Integral to their accounts is that logic (like geometry) is an axiomatic science, based on foundational truths or axioms. Such axioms Frege and Russell regarded as self-evidently true propositions, although neither of them gave a satisfactory explanation of self-evidence and how it could be objectively appealed to.[10] By

---

[9] Although 'reminder' is a term from the later Wittgenstein, remarks such as those just quoted from the *Notebooks* (NB: 11/MS 101: 39r) seem to justify its application to Wittgenstein's early philosophy too. This doesn't mean that reminders in Wittgenstein's early and late philosophy mean exactly the same. The later Wittgenstein criticizes the *Tractatus* for hypothetical theorizing, instead of only saying what everyone knows (see Kuusela 2011; cf. McGinn 2006: 32–3).

[10] The problem is that what one person regards as self-evident, another might not. What is seen as self-evident may also vary over history. Self-evidence, therefore, seems to be a merely psychological or sociological notion. (Russell tried to account for it in terms of non-inferential intuitive knowledge, but eventually abandoned the attempt.)

contrast, however, if thinkers/language users already know the principles of logic, there's no need to postulate any self-evident truths as the foundation of logic. Since the principles of logic are already known and relied upon by thinkers and speakers in practice, they require no justification in the sense of appeal to their self-evidence, although they may require clarification. About self-evidence Wittgenstein remarks: 'Self-evidence, of which Russell has said so much, can only be discarded in logic by language itself preventing every logical mistake' (TLP 5.4731).

Further, Wittgenstein uses the notion of logic as something already known to explain the a priori status of logic, that is, its independence from experience and experiential knowledge: 'That logic is a priori consists in the fact that we cannot think illogically' (TLP 5.4731). Logic is a priori in that its principles are always already assumed and relied upon in all thinking, including all experience and judgements regarding the empirical world. The principles of logic thus structure all thought and experience. If this were not the case, a mental occurrence couldn't qualify as an experience of a fact, because without logical structure it couldn't be an object of thought or enter an inference as a premise. Likewise, the possibility of inferring one thought from others presupposes that they are logically structured. Hence, we must assume that thoughts and experience already possess a logical structure, and this can't be anything imposed on them by logicians.[11]

We are now in a position to see why Wittgenstein thinks there can't be any true/false propositions or theses about logic. Insofar as in the study of logic we are concerned with the logical structure of thought and language, we are concerned with something fundamental undergirding the possibility of true/false propositions and theses, or the expression of sense and propositional content (cf. TLP 3.34–3.3421). This means that any propositions/theses about logic already presuppose what they ought to clarify, that is, the principles of logic on which their own possibility depends. Propositions or theses about logic thus, so to speak, arrive too late on the scene of clarification, and can't clarify what they are intended to clarify. Consequently, logic can't be understood as a discipline that puts forward theses with the purpose of logical clarification.

---

[11] Wittgenstein's conception of logic as something always already assumed in thinking and language use stands in contrast with the slightly later views of philosophers such as Carnap and Quine who regard logic as comparable to a scientific theory that can be adopted, as if the adoption of one logical system rather than another didn't require thinking and already presuppose logic. Thus, they don't recognize the special status of the principles of logic in comparison to scientific principles that Wittgenstein emphasizes. Still, Carnap and Quine would agree with Wittgenstein's account of the contentlessness of logic, which Carnap mentions as a key insight he got from Wittgenstein, and which distinguishes contemporary model theoretic accounts of logic from Fregean–Russellian logic (Carnap 1963: 25). (I will come to the contentlessness of logic in due course.)

This point can be explained with reference to what Wittgenstein calls his 'fundamental thought' or 'basic idea' (*Grundgedanke*), that is, his rejection of the idea that logical constants, such as the logical connectives 'and', 'or', 'not' in Frege's and Russell's systems, could be objects of true/false representation. They can't, since in representing or in taking anything as an object of thought, we already rely on logic, including the logical constants. Hence, logic, as the foundation of all representation, can't itself be an object of representation. As Wittgenstein says: 'My fundamental idea is that the "logical constants" do not represent. That the logic of the facts cannot be represented' (TLP 4.0312; cf. 5.4; NB: 37/Ms102: 58 r). The point also applies to Fregean–Russellian logical axioms. Understood as true propositions, the axioms already presuppose what they are meant to constitute a foundation for, that is, logic. Hence, logic can't be understood as an axiomatic science in the Fregean–Russellian sense.[12]

Likewise propositions about essential necessities, or internal properties generally, such as 'blue is a colour', already presuppose what they seem to be assertions about. Anyone who knows what blue is knows that it's a colour, and thus the proposition is empty of any content. According to Wittgenstein, such statements are to be understood as formal pseudo-propositions which can't be expressed in a correct logical language (TLP 5.534). Although, owing to their grammatical structure, they look like proper propositions about external properties, such as 'the chair is blue', pseudo-propositions of this kind don't constitute genuine attributions of property or genuine instances of concept application. Rather, the proper expression for pseudo-concepts such as 'colour', 'object', 'name', 'proposition', and so on, is a variable which marks the relevant logical category or form (TLP 4.127–4.1272). How such formal concepts are clarified is explained in the next section, which outlines Wittgenstein's alternative to Frege's and Russell's philosophies of logic.

1.2 The Non-substantiality of Logic and the Proper Way to Express Logical Necessity

Both acknowledging his debt to Frege and Russell and expressing his critical attitude towards their accounts of logic, Wittgenstein writes about the notion of a logical language:

---

[12] The situation is different if axioms are understood not as true propositions but as rules that define the notions of a logical system. The *Tractatus* doesn't imply any objection to such a view, since here axioms don't constitute an independently established/justified foundation consisting of true propositions in the style of metaphysical foundations. Note that, in the preceding, no appeal was made to Wittgenstein's account of language or the so-called picture theory as the ground and justification of his rejection of propositions/theses about logic (cf. Note 7).

In order to avoid these errors ['the most fundamental confusions' 'of which all of philosophy is full'; TLP 3.324, cf. 3.323], we must employ a symbolism which excludes them, by not using the same sign for different symbols and by not using in the same way signs which signify in different ways. A symbolism, that is to say, which obeys the rules of *logical* grammar – of logical syntax.

(The logical symbolism of Frege and Russell is such a language, which, however, does still not exclude all errors.) (TLP 3.325; my square brackets)

This remark indicates how the early Wittgenstein saw his task. Whilst broadly agreeing with Frege's and Russell's ideas about logic and their logic-based approach to philosophy, he set out to solve the problems pertaining to their accounts of logic and logical languages with the purpose of helping to make possible the envisaged philosophical progress. For Wittgenstein, however, an account of logic isn't articulated in terms of theses, but by devising a logical language, notation, or symbolism that makes perspicuous the logical principles underlying the expression of thought or propositions. Accordingly, the criterion of correctness for an account of logic isn't the truth of any logical theses or their correspondence with any logical facts. Rather, 'we are in possession of the correct logical conception when everything finally adds up in our symbolism [*Zeichensprache*]' (TLP 4.1213). A correct account of logic, in other words, is characterized by the absence of anomalies, such as Wittgenstein identified as affecting Frege's and Russell's logical languages (see Section 1.3). By contrast, having developed a logical language free of logical errors, thus achieving the correct logical conception, we can avoid any logical or philosophical confusions by thinking, expressing ourselves, and analysing language use in terms of this logical language. As we shall see, this view about the proper way of articulating an account of logic implies a radical break with Frege's and Russell's philosophies of logic.

Regarding the non-substantiality or contentlessness of logic, Wittgenstein wrote to Russell in the summer of 1912: 'Logic must turn out to be a TOTALLY different kind than any other science' (CL: 15). This point is echoed in the *Tractatus*: 'The correct explanation of logical propositions must give them a unique position among all propositions' (TLP 6.112; cf. NB: 107). Here Wittgenstein also connects the point about uniqueness with the non-substantiality of logic: 'Theories which make a proposition of logic appear substantial are always false' (TLP 6.111). Relatedly, he rejects Russell's account that the characteristic mark of logical propositions is their generality. As Wittgenstein points out, by generalizing propositions we don't yet express anything merely formal. This requires abstracting from all content and focusing on the use of signs rather than what they speak about (NB: 17/MS 101: 58r).[13] Moreover, as Wittgenstein points out, generality is merely accidental. Logic, by contrast, is concerned with what is necessary and essential to thought and language (TLP 6.1231–6.1232, 6.124). But if not in terms of propositions/theses, how is logic clarified?

Here we come to Wittgenstein's crucial modification of Frege's and Russell's accounts of logic. Rather than in terms of propositions or logical theses, the principles of logic are to be clarified by devising a logical language that renders them perspicuous (TLP 6.1–6.111, 6.12, 6.124). This, then, is the proper way to express what is essential or logically necessary. Although the logical or formal features of language/thought can't be an object of true/false propositions/theses, they can be clarified by means of a symbolism into whose structure they are encoded, and which consequently, unlike colloquial language, clearly shows the logical features of language/thought (TLP 4.12–4.1274; see quotations at the start of this section). (Colloquial language isn't logically perspicuous in this sense, because it serves various needs of human life and psychology, other than logical clarity (TLP 4.002).) A logical symbolism or language, by contrast, wears its logical features on its sleeve and 'obeys the rules of *logical* grammar' in this sense (TLP 3.325; quoted above).[14] It's also noteworthy how this account reflects the status of logic as something that is always already assumed and precedes the possibility of articulating thoughts or propositions, as noted in the previous section. Inasmuch as they are encoded into the structure of language, the logically necessary features of language underlie the possibility of articulating propositions. From this point of view it's then easy to see how attempts to articulate what is logically necessary in terms of propositions already presuppose what they are meant to clarify.

It's characteristic of the logical notation envisaged in the *Tractatus* then, for example, that in this notation it's possible to express a proposition only in a way that makes it evident that it possesses what Wittgenstein calls 'the general propositional form', and which he regards as constituting the essence of propositions and language as the totality of propositions (TLP 4.5, 5.471). If it's

---

[13] Wittgenstein thus replaces Russell's notion of the formality of logic with a stricter one (TLP 3.331). Notably, for Wittgenstein, syntax is an abstraction from the meaningful use of language (TLP 3.326–3.33). Thus, his notion of syntax differs from the contemporary one that regards syntactic structures as abstract structures to be given a semantic interpretation.

[14] Unlike Frege and Russell, Wittgenstein doesn't consider natural languages to be logically defective. Hence, a logical language for him doesn't constitute an improvement on natural language in the sense that only the logical language would be governed by the rules of logical syntax. In order to be able to represent reality, natural language must already be logically in order as it is (TLP 5.5563). The sense in which natural language doesn't obey logical syntax is then only that natural language conceals the logical function of its expressions. Accordingly, a main difference of Wittgenstein's logical language from natural languages is its logical perspicuity.

correct, as Wittgenstein claims in 4.5, that any possible proposition/sense can be expressed in terms of the *Tractatus'* notation – that is, every possible proposition/sense can be expressed within the constraints of the general propositional form – it's been shown that all propositions do indeed have such a common form. On this account, propositions then are true/false representations of reality that represent contingent states of affairs. Any possible proposition is either a representation of a logically simple state of affairs or a truth-function of such representations (TLP 4.5–4.53, 5, 6). But how can this account be understood as non-substantial, as not involving a substantial metaphysical claim about propositions?

With regard to Wittgenstein's view of the non-substantiality of logic, it's important that he supports his account of the essence of language and thought by merely formal considerations. As he points out, it's characteristic of propositions that any proposition can be combined with its negation so as to constitute a tautology, whereby its truth no longer depends on how the world is, that is, on the obtaining of the state of affairs that the proposition represents. Rather, the proposition is true in all circumstances, as illustrated by 'It's raining or it's not raining', which says nothing about the weather. This possibility of turning any proposition that represents reality into one that doesn't represent, Wittgenstein maintains, shows that propositions have certain formal features, that is, that they all share the general propositional form and are all true/false representations (TLP 4.6–4.61, 6.12–6.121).

Wittgenstein's view of the non-substantiality of logic is also connected with the ideals of simplicity and foreseeability of logic emphasized by him which couldn't be satisfied by means of substantial theses. A logical account must be simple because logic sets the standard for simplicity and clarity (TLP 5.4541, 5.5563). Accordingly, such an account must render logic clear and foreseeable, and exclude any surprises (TLP 6.1251). This goes for the notion of the general propositional form too. A correct logical account must exclude the possibility that we could come across propositions that wouldn't have this form. 'That there is a general form is proved by the fact that there can't be a proposition whose form could not have been foreseen (i.e. constructed)' (TLP 4.5).

The requirements of simplicity and foreseeability help to explain how Wittgenstein intends to avoid theses and to uphold his claim about the non-substantiality of logic. Rather than a thesis, the general propositional form is merely a rule for the use of signs (*Zeichenregel*). It constitutes a rule for the construction of propositions and, in this capacity, the only logical constant in Wittgenstein's logical language and its core notion. (In his logical language the general propositional form is expressed as a propositional variable. Every possible proposition is a substitution instance of this variable; TLP 4.5–4.53.) Assuming that his logical language 'excludes all mistakes' and that 'everything adds up' in it (TLP 3.325, 4.1213), Wittgenstein's logical language then makes evident that every possible proposition conforms to this rule, in that there's no other way to express a proposition in this language. Assuming that it's possible to express any possible proposition in Wittgenstein's notation, any other putative propositional forms have been excluded. With this rule, Wittgenstein therefore seems able to describe every possible proposition in terms of their essential features, but without making substantial, unforeseeable claims and without putting forward a thesis that assumes what it's meant to clarify. As he also explains: 'We can foresee only what we ourselves construct' (TLP 5.556). 'In logic process and result are equivalent. (Hence the absence of surprises.)' (TLP 6.1262). Process and result are equivalent in the case of the general propositional form in that by spelling out this rule for the construction of propositions Wittgenstein has at once formally described every possible proposition. All possible results of constructing propositions are already contained in this rule – or so the early Wittgenstein thought.[15]

The general idea of Wittgenstein's approach to logic can consequently be summed up by means of his metaphor: the logical symbolism constitutes a mirror whose purpose is to enable us to see clearly the logical principles that natural language disguises. As this brings out, the point of constructing a logical symbolism is to clarify something that isn't a human construction; that is, the logical structure of thought, language, and reality. Accordingly, Wittgenstein remarks, raising a question about the significance of the specialized signs and sign-systems introduced by logicians: 'How can the all-embracing logic which mirrors the world use such special crotchets and manipulations? Only because they are all connected with one another in an infinitely fine network, the great mirror' (TLP 5.511; cf. TLP 4.12–4.1212). 'Logic is not a doctrine but a mirror-image of the world' (TLP 6.13). '[I]n logic it is not we who express what we want by means of signs, but in logic the essence of the naturally necessary signs [*die Natur der Naturnotwendigen Zeichen*] asserts itself' (TLP 6.124). A fundamental task for logicians therefore is to devise a notation in which logic can find a clear expression, thus bringing into the open what natural language disguises and by so doing explicating the

---

[15] As he realizes later on, in connection with what is known as the colour exclusion problem, the *Tractatus*' account of truth-functions can't account for the logical behaviour of all propositions; that is, for the exclusion of propositions such as 'this object is red and green all over', the possibility of which is permanently, not merely contingently, excluded. In this truth-table there's consequently a line missing in comparison with normal truth-tables (see RLF).

logical knowledge that thinkers and language users already possess. Equipped with such a language, we can then pursue philosophy as logical analysis and leave behind metaphysical theses that attempt to state in propositional form what propositions can't express.

1.3 Logical Consequence and Other Improvements on Fregean–Russellian Logic

The preceding considerations also inform Wittgenstein's account of logical consequence. Similarly to his rejection of the view of logic as a science that establishes substantial theses/truths, his account of inference is based on the insight that in order for linguistic agents to be able to think/speak they must already grasp the principles of logic. Thus, it isn't for logicians to decide what counts as a valid inference but this depends on thought and language themselves: logic takes care of itself. Here Wittgenstein's position again contrasts with those of Frege and Russell, who assume that logical axioms, understood as self-evident, necessarily true logical propositions, are needed to justify logical inferences. Wittgenstein, by contrast, thinks that whatever licences inferring one proposition from other propositions must already be contained in the propositions themselves. He writes:

If p follows from q, I can conclude from q to p; infer p from q.
The method of inference is to be understood from the two propositions alone.
Only they themselves can justify the inference.
   Laws of inference, which – as in Frege and Russell – are to justify the conclusions, are senseless and would be superfluous. (TLP 5.132)

On Wittgenstein's account, there's therefore no need for axioms or rules of inference established by logicians. If an inference from q to p is justified, its justification depends on the propositions that are part of the inference. Insofar as these propositions possess determinate logical forms – without which they wouldn't be propositions – this suffices to determine whether p can be inferred from q. Inference, in other words, depends on the formal features of the propositions involved in the inference, not on any additional propositions, such as Fregean–Russellian axioms (TLP 5.13, 5.131). One advantage of this view, then, is that it releases Wittgenstein from the regress-problem raised by Lewis Carroll, the nub of which is that treating rules of inference or axioms as true propositions that figure as additional premises in inferences, as Frege and Russell do, does nothing to help to justify inferences. For just as one can ask about the original premises what licenses the transition from them to the conclusion, and maintain that this should be secured by an additional premise licensing the inference, one can ask the same question about any extended set of premises where logical axioms figure as propositions playing the role of extra premises. Hence, if axioms are regarded as true propositions, adding them as extra premises to inferences can't explain the legitimacy of inferences. This merely gives rise to an infinite regress (see Carroll 1895; cf. VW: 179ff.).

A related feature of Wittgenstein's account is that logical propositions are ultimately not essential to logic, contrary to Frege and Russell. They are merely an aid that helps to confirm the validity of inferences. Given that propositions involved in a valid inference jointly constitute a tautology, as Wittgenstein maintains, the validity of an inference can be confirmed by establishing the tautologousness of the set of propositions. However, because the tautologousness of a set of propositions can also be seen immediately in a perspicuous logical notation, this procedure isn't necessary. 'From this it follows that we can get on without logical propositions, for in an adequate notation we can recognize the formal properties of the propositions by mere inspection' (TLP 6.122). 'Proof in logic is only a mechanical expedient to facilitate the recognition of tautology, where it is complicated' (TLP 6.1262). Accordingly, 'if we know the logical syntax of any sign language, then all the propositions of logic are already given' (TLP 6.124). (Wittgenstein also provides, for cases where generality is not involved, a notational device whose purpose is to help establish the tautologousness of a set of propositions (TLP 6.1203).)

Here it's significant that what counts as a proposition of logic can be recognized from the symbols alone, without appeal to any substantial truths. This point, Wittgenstein maintains, 'contains in itself the whole philosophy of logic' (TLP 6.113; cf. 6.126). Logic, in other words, isn't an area of study where we establish substantial truths or theses about the nature of thought, language, and the world. Neither does the validity of inferences depend on such truths. This is again connected with Wittgenstein's 'fundamental thought' that logic doesn't put forward any propositions/theses about the logical or formal features of thought/language. Rather, as noted, the study of logic clarifies the logical features of thought/language by giving them a clear expression.

In addition to the preceding ways of reconceiving Frege's and Russell's accounts of logic, Wittgenstein proposes solutions to a variety of more specific problems that arise for them, so as to improve their notations with a view to achieving a conception where 'everything adds up in our symbolism'. Here a few examples will have to suffice. For example, Wittgenstein clarifies the difference between names and propositions, which is left unclear in Frege and Russell, emphasizing that only propositions have a truth-value and that, unlike names, an articulate structure is essential to propositions (TLP 3.142–3.144, 4.032). He also solves Russell's problems of the unity of propositions and the possibility of false propositions. On Wittgenstein's account no 'cement', such as

Russell tried to identify (for example, as provided by the acts of the mind), is needed to account for the unity of propositions; that is, how the names in a proposition constitute a unified judgeable thought/proposition. This isn't needed because Tractarian names (like Fregean functions and arguments) can only occur in combination with one another, never separately, in accordance with Frege's context-principle. Thus the possibility of their combination with other names is a built-in feature of Tractarian names, in the absence of which an expression couldn't count as a name (TLP 3.3, 4.23).[16] Moreover, propositions can represent what isn't the case, because they only represent possible states of affairs, asserting but not implying the actuality of what is represented. In this they differ from propositions on Russell's theories of judgement which, by implying the actuality of what is thought or spoken of, fail to account for the possibility of false propositions (TLP 4.031–4.0311).[17] Likewise Wittgenstein solves a problem that arises for Frege's account of negation as a second-level function. Whilst a doubly-negated thought in Frege is meant to be equivalent with the original thought (as exemplified by p, ¬¬p, ¬¬¬¬p, and so on), in Frege's system it's in fact a new function that expresses a new thought, created by applying the function of negation to the original function. This leaves it unclear why it should be equivalent with the original thought. By contrast, in the *Tractatus* the operation of negation can cancel itself out (TLP 5.43–5.44). This solves the Fregean anomaly regarding negation.

1.4 Interpretations of the *Tractatus* and How Its Presumed Paradox Is Solved

As I have presented the *Tractatus'* account of logic, Wittgenstein works from within Frege's and Russell's approaches, addressing tensions and inconsistencies in their accounts. Notably, this isn't how Wittgenstein's early philosophy has been traditionally interpreted. Instead, his rejection of logical theses and the account of logic as a science have often been regarded as the consequences of his own picture theory of propositions or language, according to which

---

[16] This doesn't mean that any name can be combined with any other. On Wittgenstein's account possible/sensible propositions correspond to what is logically possible, with a correct logical language excluding the construction of any nonsensical sentences.

[17] These points about the difference between names and propositions, the unity of propositions, and the possibility of false propositions are clarified in the *Tractatus* by means of the so-called picture theory of propositions. Instead of being construed as a nonsensical theory, however, Wittgenstein's account of propositions as pictures is arguably better understood as a further clarification of the principles governing a correct logical language. Its purpose thus is to explicate something assumed by the notion of general propositional form, that is, how names and propositions symbolize. Accordingly, as with Wittgenstein's other logical insights, the proper expression for his account of propositions as pictures is a logical notation based on relevant principles, not the sentences of the *Tractatus*. See Kuusela, forthcoming.

propositions represent contingent states of affairs and therefore can't say anything about what is logically necessary. (See for instance Anscombe 1971 and Hacker 1986. Kuusela 2021 and forthcoming provide critical discussions and an alternative interpretation.) Hence, traditional *Tractatus*-interpretations envisage Wittgenstein as arguing against Frege and Russell from the point of view of his own theory of propositions, which neither is committed to accept. This makes it unclear why Frege and Russell should care, and portrays Wittgenstein's argumentation strategy as dogmatic. (Wittgenstein is here taken to argue dogmatically from within his own position, rather than addressing the problems with the accounts he's arguing against from within those accounts.)

Notoriously, such an interpretation also construes the *Tractatus* as containing a paradox, with Wittgenstein arguing for the rejection of logical theses on the basis of his own thesis about the nature of thought/language. For insofar as his thesis about language can show the impossibility of other theses, it paradoxically appears that theses are possible after all. (The paradox is simple to formulate: if the *Tractatus* contains a thesis/theory, it can't be nonsense; if it's nonsense, it can't contain a thesis/theory.) Given Wittgenstein's view of the impossibility of truths and theses about logic, it has then also seemed necessary to some interpreters to postulate a category of ineffable truths about the nature of thought, language, and reality that can't be stated or entertained but which somehow nevertheless support and justify the claim about the impossibility of propositions about logic (Hacker 1986 and 2000). This is problematic, however, not only because of the oxymoronic notion of a truth/thesis that can't be entertained but can nevertheless be recognized as true. It's problematic also because Wittgenstein's commitment to such ineffable theses or truths makes it unclear how the *Tractatus* could meet the requirements of the foreseeability and contentlessness of logic, given that Wittgenstein is now understood as putting forward a substantial thesis of his own about the nature of propositions and language. (The attribution of ineffable truths or necessities is also exegetically problematic because Wittgenstein never mentions any such notion. Neither does he ever describe the *Tractatus* as containing a paradox. Its attribution to the *Tractatus* therefore lacks any direct textual evidence.) As we have seen, however, there's no need to read Wittgenstein in this problematic way. It's perfectly possible to understand the *Tractatus* consistently with its own principles.

Importantly, the preceding problems with the traditional interpretations, including the paradox, are dissolved if the *Tractatus* is read as aiming to introduce a logical notation that constitutes the proper expression of his logical insights. Now there's no paradox, in that to introduce a logical language isn't the same as putting forward any propositions/theses about logic. (A language or a notation doesn't constitute a thesis about anything.) Accordingly, rather than constituting propositions/theses, the sentences of the *Tractatus* can be understood as serving the purpose of introducing the formal concepts and principles of Wittgenstein's logical language. Here, then, it's important that, if Wittgenstein's purpose is only to clarify what thinkers/speakers already know, there's no need for any propositions/theses that purport to inform them about the logical principles governing thought/language. His readers, who are thinkers/ language users and thus already tacitly know the principles of logic, can meet Wittgenstein 'half-way' (cf. Frege 1966a: 54). That is, relying on their already extant comprehension of logic, they are in principle in a position to understand what Wittgenstein is trying to get at with his sentences, and also to judge for themselves whether to accept his language as rendering perspicuous the principles of logic they already know. The alleged paradox can thus be dissolved by reconceiving the role of the sentences of *Tractatus* in a manner that doesn't treat them as theses. Consequently the paradox no longer hounds the *Tractatus* as a major anomaly that led Russell to comment on its plausibility or acceptability: 'What causes hesitation is the fact that, after all, Mr Wittgenstein manages to say a good deal about what cannot be said' (TLP 22). On the proposed account Wittgenstein makes no such mistake (see Kuusela 2019c: chapters 2 and 3, and 2021 for a more detailed discussion).[18]

To relate the proposed interpretation to others, it should be evident from the preceding that it stands in contrast with the traditional metaphysical interpretations, represented by Anscombe and Hacker among others, that ascribe nonsensical theses or ineffable truths to the *Tractatus*, which consequently gives rise to the alleged paradox. Instead, the interpretation presented here can be classified as a version of what is known as the resolute reading, originally developed by Cora Diamond and James Conant, and characterized by two

---

[18] As Carnap, too, recognized later (1937/1967), it's perfectly possible to introduce logical principles and formal concepts by means of sentences that seem to constitute substantial propositions about reality but are really used to explain the principles and the role of formal concepts in a logical notation. An example is 'A name means an object; the object is its meaning' (TLP 3.203), which employs the formal concepts of a name and object as if they were proper concepts. This creates the appearance of the sentence expressing a proposition/thesis about the nature of names, but it can also be readily construed as indicating the logical role of names in Wittgenstein's notation: in this notation names are referring expressions and the objects of reference their meanings. The same goes for sentences like 'The elementary proposition consists of names' (TLP 4.22), which explains the relationship between the formal concepts of a name and proposition. *Mutatis mutandis* for other Tractarian sentences, including the ones at the beginning concerning ontology. In short, the *Tractatus*' ontology of objects and facts is a counterpart of its logical language. Looked at from the point of view of the notation expressive of the correct logical conception, the world is a totality of facts that consist of objects in combination, and so on (TLP 1ff.). Thus, we reach the same general point again: Wittgenstein's notation, not the sentences of the *Tractatus*, constitutes the proper expression for his philosophical views (see Kuusela 2019c, chapter 3).

commitments that I have relied on in the preceding: 1) the rejection of ineffable truths and 2) that Wittgenstein's purpose is only to clarify what thinkers/ speakers already know. (For these two commitments of the resolute reading, see Conant and Bronzo 2017.)

Resolute readings in this precise sense also contrast with certain other interpretations under the same name. Characteristic of the latter is that they regard the *Tractatus* as merely aiming to reveal the nonsensicality of philosophical theorizing by demonstrating to its readers how its own theories collapse into nonsense. Warren Goldfarb explains: 'A resolute view has to say, if we truly throw the ladder away, how is it that the nonsense could have been helpful. . . . The answer must lie in this: in showing that there is no such thing as an ontological theory, one should give the best ontological theory one can find, and show its terms fall apart upon closer logical inspection. Similarly with a theory of propositions' (Goldfarb 1997: 71). Even though interpretations of this kind, often described as therapeutic albeit Goldfarb doesn't use this word, can explain what it is for Wittgenstein not to have theses, they suffer from another problem. If Wittgenstein's only aim is that his readers should recognize the nonsensicality of his presumed theories and by extension the nonsensicality of philosophical theorizing, it becomes unclear how the book could be understood as making a positive contribution to logic or the philosophy thereof. As Hacker puts it, the resolute reading risks throwing away the baby of logic with the bathwater of nonsense (Hacker 2000: 369). This risk seems realized in the case of resolute readings in Goldfarb's or the therapeutic sense. Interpretations that regard the book as merely aiming to reveal its own nonsensicality appear to lack the resources to explain how Wittgenstein could express any specific positive logical insights. How, in that case, is Wittgenstein able to express and communicate to the readers his views about logic? By contrast, the proposed reading can readily answer Goldfarb's question about the purpose of nonsense *and* explain how Wittgenstein's logical insights are retained after the *Tractatus'* sentences have been discarded as nonsense. As explained, the purpose of the *Tractatus'* sentences is to introduce the principles and formal concepts constitutive of a logical language. This language, not the book's nonsensical sentences, is the proper expression for Wittgenstein's logical insights. (Goldfarb considers an answer along these lines but rejects it, maintaining – very strangely in my view – that there's no logical language, or a specification of its concepts and principles, to be found in the *Tractatus*; Goldfarb 1997: 72.)

Here it's also noteworthy that, problematically, the metaphysical and therapeutic interpretations seem to tacitly share the assumption that the only way to express positive insights about logic is philosophical propositions/theses.

Whilst the metaphysical interpretation maintains that unless Wittgenstein has such theses he can't provide a positive account of logic, the therapeutic reading maintains that owing to his rejection of theses no positive account of logic can be ascribed to the *Tractatus* (Read and Deans 2003 and 2011). Thus, both interpretations beg the question against Wittgenstein's attempt to abandon theses. As we have seen, however, the *Tractatus* can be read in a way that does justice to its attempt to leave behind philosophical theses. No theses are needed to introduce the logical language into the structure of which Wittgenstein's account of logic is encoded. (For a criticism of the metaphysical and therapeutic readings, see Kuusela 2019a.)

Although the support needed for the proposed interpretation can be found in the *Tractatus* and other pre-Tractarian texts (notebooks and correspondence), upon his return to philosophy in 1929, Wittgenstein explicitly stated as his own the view that a notation constitutes the ultimate expression for a philosophical view. He writes, commenting on Frank Ramsey: 'R doesn't understand the value that I place on a particular notation, ... because he doesn't see that therein is articulated a whole way of looking at the object of study; .... The notation is the last expression of a philosophical view' (MS 105: 10–12). Of course, this view can't simply be read back into the *Tractatus*. Arguably, however, various remarks in the book support the interpretation that Wittgenstein already held this view there (Kuusela 2019a). Further support is provided by Wittgenstein's later comments and criticisms of the *Tractatus* (see Section 2).

Finally, if Wittgenstein isn't putting forward any theses, how can he say that 'the truth of thoughts communicated here seems to me unassailable and definitive' (preface)? Presumably the thoughts communicated in the book relate to the issue of how to account for logic and how to approach logical and philosophical questions without falling into the widespread confusion of philosophy regarding internal and external properties. Of the truth of an account of logic Wittgenstein says:

> All propositions of our colloquial language are actually, just as they are, logically completely in order. That most simple thing which we ought to give here isn't a simile of truth but the complete truth itself.
>
> (Our problems are not abstract but perhaps the most concrete that there are.) (TLP 5.5563)

What the book aims to communicate is therefore indeed a truth, although this isn't anything expressible by means of theses or propositions but is more fundamental than that. This truth is expressed by designing a logical language that renders perspicuous the principles of logic disguised by natural language, that is, by codifying relevant principles into the structure of a logical language.

It's thus a truth expressed by means of a notation intended to mirror logic and to give it a perspicuous expression. This is what the reader is expected to grasp and then hold on to after throwing away Wittgenstein's sentences that introduce the concepts and principles of his notation. As Wittgenstein says at the end of the book:

> My sentences elucidate in this way: he who understands me finally recognizes them as nonsense, when he has climbed out through them, on them, over them. (He must so to speak throw away the ladder, after he has climbed up on it.)
>
> He must surmount these sentences; then he sees the world aright. (TLP 6.54)

On the proposed interpretation Wittgenstein's sentences can indeed be thrown away. Their purpose was only to introduce the formal concepts and principles of a logical language expressive of the correct logical conception, and after the reader has understood the idea of this language, his sentences are no longer needed. Accordingly, the sentences can now be recognized as nonsense in that they are not expressible in the correct logical language. Thus, insofar as Wittgenstein's language 'adds up', giving expression to the correct logical conception and rendering logic perspicuous, it also renders perspicuous why the Tractarian sentences can't be construed as propositions/theses. From this point of view – that is, the point of view of a correct logical conception embodied in Wittgenstein's notation – the reader can then finally see the world aright. Now they are also in a position to start philosophizing in the 'strictly correct' way by engaging in logical analysis, with Wittgenstein's notation providing a framework for such analyses (TLP 6.53). This intriguing view of what it is to express logical and philosophical views Wittgenstein comes to both criticize and develop further in his later philosophy.

2 Later Wittgenstein's Rethinking of the *Tractatus'* Philosophy of Logic

In the preface to the *Investigations* Wittgenstein says that he came to 'recognize grave mistakes' in the *Tractatus*. As I noted in the introduction, it's controversial to what extent his early and later philosophy are continuous; that is, whether the later Wittgenstein rejects the *Tractatus'* account of logic and language or radically rethinks its approach to logic and philosophy, continuing to build on its key insights. This means that it's controversial what his grave mistakes were. Is it a mistake, for example, that he regarded language as a calculus? Did his mistakes require him to start completely anew or to revise and develop further the insights of his early book?

That Wittgenstein makes a new start is suggested by the fact that in his later work he often describes himself as engaged in a grammatical rather than a logical investigation (PI §90). This, however, is too weak to support the discontinuity thesis on which Wittgenstein rejects the *Tractatus* rather than builds on it. There are many examples of him using the terms 'grammar' and 'logic' (and other related expressions) interchangeably or nearly interchangeably. The close connection between the two is evident after Wittgenstein's return to philosophy in 1929, when he begins to use the term 'grammar' instead of 'logic' or 'syntax', but in a way similar to his earlier use of 'logic'. For example, he says that grammar spells out logical distinctions and grammatical rules determine the role of variables (MS 108: 153). Grammar shows what is logically possible (MS 140: 8/PG: 45; BB: 56) and clarifies what follows from a sentence (MS 109: 15). Logical problems and questions are said to be grammatical (MS 109: 224/TS 211: 398; Z §590), and logical analysis is characterized as the clarification of grammar (PR: 51/MS: 108, 88/TS 209: 1/TS 213: 417). Around this time Wittgenstein sums up his view by saying: 'I always want to show that what is business about logic must be said in grammar' (MS 109: 122). Thus, although the notion of grammar in the later Wittgenstein is broader than that of logic in the *Tractatus*, grammar covers everything that logic did (being in this sense interchangeable or partly interchangeable). This use of 'grammar' and 'logic' then seems to continue throughout Wittgenstein's philosophical career (MS 138: 17b; MS 157a: 54v; MS 167: 26r; TS 233a: 38; TS 245: 310/RPP I §1050). For example, the use of 'logic' is prevalent in *On Certainty*, based on excerpts from Wittgenstein's last manuscripts. Here he connects language-games with logic as follows: 'everything that describes a language-game belongs to logic' (MS 172: 18/OC §56; cf. §§82, 628). Wittgenstein therefore doesn't seem to draw any principled distinction between logic and grammar that would justify any strict separation or break between logic and grammar.[19] But what then are the grave mistakes Wittgenstein found in the *Tractatus*?

2.1 Confusing the Mode and Object of Representation: Idealization and Abstraction

In the *Investigations* Wittgenstein describes the *Tractatus* as having confused the features of a mode or a form representation – that is, the logical language or calculus envisaged in the *Tractatus* – with the features of the object of

---

[19] See Kuusela 2011 for discussion of what Wittgenstein means by saying that his new thoughts put forward in the *Investigations* 'could be seen in the right light only by contrast with and against the background of my older way of thinking' (PI: preface).

study – that is, thought and language whose logical features Wittgenstein's language was intended to explicate. 'One predicates of the thing what lies in the mode of representation. We take the possibility of comparison, which impresses us, as the perception of a highly general state of affairs' (PI §104). What he means by the impressive comparison, I take it, is the comparison between language and calculi, which in certain ways is indeed very impressive (cf. PI §81). (To be sure, many philosophers have found it so, and many continue to think of language as if it were a calculus.)

Wittgenstein connects this confusion with the *Tractatus*' account of the general propositional form: '*Tractatus Logico-Philosophicus* (4.5): "The general form of propositions is: This is how things are." — That is the kind of proposition [*Satz*] one repeats to oneself countless times. One thinks that one is tracing nature over and over again, and one is merely tracing round the frame through which we look at it' (PI §114). Connecting these remarks also with the next one, 'A *picture* held us captive' (PI §115), Wittgenstein's point can be explained as follows. His early account of thought, language, and logic relied on a picture based on a comparison of thought and language with a truth-functional calculus. Whilst such a calculus may constitute a helpful mode of representing and clarifying the function of thought and language for certain purposes, Wittgenstein failed to recognize it for what it is, that is, a mode or a form of representation or a model that *he* was using to describe the object of investigation of logic. (Recall the *Tractatus*' aspiration to articulate not merely a simile of truth but the whole truth; TLP 5.5563.) Instead he confused the features of his mode of representation with the features of the object of investigation which led him to make simplistic and dogmatic claims about language and thought that failed to do justice to their manifoldness and complexity (cf. PI §23 and quotation from MS 152 in the introduction). More specifically, whilst it's characteristic of Wittgenstein's logical language that every possible proposition expressible in it has the general propositional form, he went on to claim much more ambitiously that every proposition really does have this form, believing he had got hold of the very essence of language. But in so doing he was 'merely tracing round the frame' through which he was looking at language.

As Wittgenstein also explains in an earlier version of the *Investigations* where §104 and §114 are part of a single longer remark: 'The expression of this confusion is the metaphysical use of our words' (TS 220 §110). Although the *Tractatus* was meant to leave behind metaphysical theses and to offer an account of logic and logical methodology without reliance on substantial theses, it failed to achieve this. Instead, Wittgenstein committed himself to a thesis about the nature of thought, language, and the world that involved the postulation of logical structures constitutive of the underlying hidden logical structure of thought and language which his calculus was intended to mirror. For although one is not committed to any theses by simply putting forward a logical language, the claim that all philosophical problems could be solved by means of the method of analysis of the *Tractatus* did commit Wittgenstein to a thesis about the nature of language; that is, that all sensible linguistic expressions can be analysed in terms of the method he had introduced. Thus, in the *Tractatus* metaphysics disguised itself as logical methodology. Consequently, it was left for the later Wittgenstein to chase metaphysics out of this 'last hiding place' (MS 110: 194; cf. Kuusela 2008: chapter 7.1 for discussion).

More specifically, because Wittgenstein's mode of representing language as a truth-functional calculus required that all propositions have a definite truth-value (since otherwise they can't be part of determinate truth-functions), he was led to postulate underlying definite and exact logical rules according to which thought and language function, and which would ensure that every proposition does have a definite truth-value. As he came to recognize later, however, this postulation involves a misunderstanding about ideal notions in logic, in particular its ideals of simplicity and exactness. Trying to satisfy the ideals of simplicity and exactness, Wittgenstein fell into what he later calls the sublimation of logic, that is, the postulation of neat abstract, ideal, and uniform logical structures, or as he also refers to them, crystalline rules, as the underlying structure of language (cf. PI §89). He writes about his confusion:

> – But I want to say: we misunderstand the role played by the ideal in our language. . . .
>   We want to say that there can't be any vagueness in logic. The idea now absorbs us that the ideal 'must' be found in reality. Meanwhile we do not as yet see how it occurs there, nor do we understand the nature of this 'must'. We think it must be in reality; for we think we already see it there.
>   The strict and clear rules for the logical construction of a proposition appear to us as something in the background – hidden in the medium of the understanding. I already see them (even though through a medium), for I understand the propositional sign, I use it to say something. (PI §§100–102)

In the *Tractatus* the ideals of simplicity and exactness were reified by postulating hidden, underlying logical structures that would satisfy them. Because natural language, owing to its complexity and vagueness, is unable to satisfy those ideals, Wittgenstein thought that satisfying them would require postulating ideal logical structures, pure from the messiness of anything empirical, at an underlying level. And since thinkers and language users must already have a grasp of logic, it seemed that this postulation was merely a matter of clarifying something they already knew, albeit 'hidden in the medium of understanding', with some kind of subconscious processes of the mind taking care of the processing of thought and language at the hidden underlying level. As explained in PI §§100–102, however, this constitutes a confusion about the role of ideal notions in logic. Or, as Wittgenstein also comments on the problem with the postulation of such underlying logical structures and corresponding processes of the mind: 'In philosophy we are always in danger of giving a mythology of the symbolism, or of psychology: instead of simply saying what everyone knows and must admit' (PR: 65; cf. PG: 56).[20]

The question, then, is whether another way can be found to satisfy the ideals of simplicity and exactness, or more generally the ideals of rigour to which simplicity and exactness contribute and which partly define logic as the study or discipline it is. Is it possible to satisfy these ideals without sublimating thought and language by postulating ideal structures? If not, that is, if rigour is bargained out of logic in this way and it's concluded that logic cannot meet the ideals of rigour, 'logic is dissolved' (PI §108, quoted below). Importantly, however, describing the problem in the preceding terms already indicates a solution. (For Wittgenstein's struggles to articulate the core of his mistake, see MS 157a and 157b from 1937.) Wittgenstein explains his solution in general terms (which also apply to philosophical theorizing more generally) as follows:

> For we can avoid unfairness or vacuity in our assertions only by presenting the model as what it is, as an object of comparison – as a sort of yardstick; not as a preconception to which reality *must* correspond. (The dogmatism into which we fall so easily in doing philosophy.) (PI §131)

The point of this remark, and how it applies to the *Tractatus*, can be explained as follows. The dogmatism and misleading simplifications of Wittgenstein's early philosophy of logic can be avoided by recognizing its account of logic and language as a model; that is, a mode of representing language use for specific purposes. Contrary to the *Tractatus*, this mode of representation ought not to be imposed onto language as a claim/thesis about what it must be, whereby it's asserted that every possible proposition must be a true/false representation or a truth-function thereof. (I return to the employment of models shortly.) The problem with the *Tractatus* thus isn't simply that it regarded language as a calculus. The problem is its failure to recognize this mode of representation

---

[20] This strategy of postulating underlying structures and mental processes continues to be popular in the philosophy of language, even if not to the same extent in logic, given the influence of Carnap's and Quine's view of logic as the design of logical languages and systems that can be adopted like a scientific theory. However, partly under the influence of Chomskyan linguistics, the *Tractatus*-style approach still also continues to exist in the context of contemporary logic and philosophy thereof (cf. Hanna 2006).

as a particular way of representing language that emphasizes some of its features at the expense of others, and can't be claimed to capture the essence of language as such. On the one hand, it's a feature of the *Tractatus'* model for language that every possible proposition has the general form. On the other hand, however, it isn't correct that whatever is true of a model, even if it's able to do important clarificatory work, must also be true about what it's a model of. The Tractarian model ought therefore not to be projected onto language as a claim/thesis about its nature and, more generally, no mode of representing language/thought or of regimenting or ordering 'our knowledge of the use of language' should be treated as *the* ultimate ordering of our knowledge of language use. Rather, as Wittgenstein emphasizes, philosophy aims to establish 'an order for a particular purpose, one out of many possible orders, not *the* order' (PI §132), whereby the purpose that such an orderings serve is achieving clarity about particular unclarities or confusions. In this regard it's then important that features of language use whose clarification and emphasis are called for to solve certain confusions might not be relevant for clarifying other, different confusions relating to the same expressions or uses of language. Contrary to the *Tractatus'* bold methodological claim, no single way of ordering our knowledge of language use can be expected to contain the solution to all problems, not even to problems relating to certain specific concepts or issues. The big programmatic claim of the early Wittgenstein about *the* method of philosophy was not justified.

The preceding, then, is the problem that Wittgenstein's later methodology and his new account of the status of logical models as 'objects of comparison' are meant to solve.

> Our clear and simple language-games are not preliminary studies for a future regimentation of language – as it were, first approximations, ignoring friction and air resistance. Rather, the language-games stand there as *objects of comparison* which, through similarities and dissimilarities, are meant to throw light on features of our language. (PI §130)

It's notable that this remark applies to logical calculi too, not just Wittgenstein's simple language-games introduced in his later work. (Language-games and other clarificatory models and methods are discussed in Section 3.) As Wittgenstein points out, any system of syntactical rules, such as a logical calculus, can be understood as a game according to rules, and as a language-game in this sense, although the contrary isn't true because the notion of a game is broader than that of a calculus (WVC: 103–5; MS 106: 139). Calculus-based logical methods, such as that of the *Tractatus*, can therefore be reinterpreted in accordance with Wittgenstein's later methodology. Importantly, however, when employed as objects of comparison, whereby both their similarities and differences from the objects of study are to be recognized, such models or modes of representation no longer involve a commitment to any theses about the nature of thought/language as a calculus, such as the *Tractatus* relapsed to. No doctrinal commitments are implied by the possibility of clarifying specific aspects of language by means of a calculus, and thus it would be a mistake to reject calculus-based logical methods on the grounds that they commit one to a simplistic thesis of language as a calculus. Crucially, in Wittgenstein's later approach, language is only *compared* to a calculus, not claimed to be one. The same considerations then also apply to simple language-games, Wittgenstein's grammatical rules, and other clarificatory models. Claiming that language actually functions like these models, for example that it's a 'motley of language-games' or that its uses must be regarded rule-governed (cf. quotations from Hacker in the introduction), runs the same risk of becoming 'a preconception to which reality *must* correspond' that was actualized in the *Tractatus*. Now the features of later Wittgenstein's clarificatory models would again be imposed on the objects of clarification in forgetfulness of what such models really are, that is, modes of representing language use. As this shows, Wittgenstein's methodological point generalizes to all logical and philosophical models, as indicated by the general formulation in §131.

It's then important for Wittgenstein's new approach that the possibility of clarifying the workings of language by means of clarificatory models, such as calculi or language-games, requires no justification by means of any foundational theses about the nature of thought/language. Rather, the models justify themselves through the clarificatory work they do in specific contexts. This eliminates the need for any theses regarding the nature of thought/language as the foundation of logic. (Metaphysics isn't needed as the basis of logic.) As Wittgenstein remarks: 'We mean all sorts of things by "proposition", and it is wrong to start with a definition of proposition and build up logic from that' – as Frege, Russell, and following them the *Tractatus* had done (AWL: 13; cf. PI §§65ff.). Contrary to what the early Wittgenstein thought, there's no single fundamental problem to be solved regarding the essence of propositions or the nature of thought/language (or the essence of the world which thought and language speak about) to establish a foundation for logic. The justification of logical methods and the clarifications given in their terms don't require laying out the nature of propositions or language 'once and for all, and independently of any future experience', but only the recognition that the methods can be used to clarify particular confusions and solve particular philosophical problems (PI §§90–92, 97; cf. NB: 39/MS 102: 63r). As Wittgenstein also explains:

We don't want to refine or complete the system of rules for the use of our words in unheard-of ways.

For the clarity that we are aiming at is indeed *complete* clarity. But this simply means that the philosophical problems should *completely* disappear.

... Instead, a method is now demonstrated by examples, and the series of examples can be broken off. — Problems are solved (difficulties eliminated), not a *single* problem. (PI §133)

Instead of making a big programmatic *Tractatus*-style claim about there being a single method of logical analysis that can be applied to any sensible instance of language use and used to solve any philosophical problem through the clarification of the logic of relevant expressions, in the *Investigations* Wittgenstein seeks to introduce several methods of logical-grammatical clarification by demonstrating by means of examples how they can be used to address philosophical problems. (In this regard it's significant that the problems discussed in the *Investigations* aren't mere illustrations or toy problems.) Contrary to what the *Tractatus* assumed, 'There is not a single method, though there are indeed methods, as it were different therapies' (PI §133). Just as in medicine and psychology different conditions require a different treatment, so in logic and philosophy different problems may require different methods to tackle them (cf. the quotation from *Remarks on Colour* in the introduction).

We are now in a position to understand Wittgenstein's explanation of how the *Tractatus'* method of logical clarification needs to be revised, and his metaphor of repositioning the crystalline rules which the *Tractatus* postulated as hidden under the surface of language and which Wittgenstein now uses to explain his new methodology. He writes: 'The preconception that lies in [the ideal of crystalline purity] can only be eliminated by turning around our whole examination; and thereby positioning that purity in a new place' (MS 157a: 67r–v, my square brackets). Similarly, he speaks of 'a regrouping' whereby the ideal of rigour 'will be recognized as part of the mode of representation' (MS 157b: 2v–3r). The *Investigations* explains the point thus:

We see that what we call 'sentence' and 'language' has not the formal unity that I imagined, but is the family of structures more or less related to one another. – But what becomes of logic now? Its rigour seems to be giving way here. – But in that case doesn't logic altogether dissolve? – For how can it lose its rigour? Of course not by our bargaining any of its rigour out of it. – The preconception of crystalline purity can only be removed by turning our whole examination round. (One might say: the axis of reference of our examination must be rotated, but on the pivot of our real need.) (PI §108)

Once the simplistic character of the *Tractatus'* account of the formal unity of language in terms of the notion of general propositional form has been recognized, the question is: What becomes of logic now? If we conclude that language is a collection of different language-games, and that all we can do is to give empirical descriptions of this complex and fluctuating variety, we will have bargained away the rigour of logic. From this point of view, language doesn't admit of simple and exact descriptions, but they are bound to misrepresent its uses as simpler and more exact than they are. Consequently, it seems that logic's ideals of rigour and clarity can't be satisfied, after all. Problematically, however, insofar as logic as a discipline is partly defined through its ideals of simplicity and exactness as ways to attain rigour and clarity, we have bargained away logic itself![21] Here is where the idea of repositioning the ideal crystalline rules or turning round the examination comes in.

Granted that the crystalline rules are recognized as a mode of representing language use or a model, we are free to present the uses of language as being as simple and exact as is needed for specific purposes of clarification. There's no problem with this as long as nothing relevant for the specific clarificatory task at hand is misrepresented and everything relevant for the task is accounted for in the chosen terms. (What features of the use of expressions are relevant for a task of clarification depends on the particular problems to be addressed and can't be determined generally in advance of their articulation.) Thus, as Wittgenstein notes in the quotation from MS 157b, the ideal of rigour is to be recognized as part of the mode or form of representation of logic. The way to satisfy the ideal of rigour, in other words, is to devise clarificatory models that satisfy it, enabling us to think of our objects of investigation in simple and exact terms and thus to attain rigour, whilst keeping in mind that our models are merely models. In this way we can clarify language in simple and exact terms without turning logic into a sublime structure pure from the messiness of the empirical world, because we are now in a position to recognize both the similarity and difference between our models and actual language use. Consequently, simplicity and exactness can serve 'our real need' for clarity, without tempting us to questionable theoretical postulations and the sublimation of logic. Following this method we can simplify by abstracting away irrelevant features of language use, and present uses as more exact or neat (exceptionless and uniform) than they are, as long as this serves the particular clarificatory tasks at hand. For example, there's no problem with representing a distinction as exact and strict in

---

[21] Simplicity is important for clarity in that what is simple can be clearly understood and perspicuously presented. Exactness can similarly serve clarity, granted that we don't misunderstand the task of making something more exact for the specific purposes of clarification as one of working towards a 'state of complete exactness' (PI §91).

order to clarify it, even if it isn't always observed in everyday language, and there are grey areas where it can't be drawn (cf. PI §77). (Wittgenstein distinguishes in this way between statements of a rule and true/false empirical statements, despite many occasions of the use of colloquial language where the distinction isn't observed and we hover between the different uses.) Similarly, features of use can be abstracted away in order to highlight general patterns of use. The important point is this: simplifying by abstracting away features of language use and idealizing by making uses of language neater and more exact are perfectly fine, as long as nothing relevant to the particular clarificatory tasks at hand is obscured.

Finally, with regard to the point in *Investigations* §130 (cf. PI §81) that simple language-games aren't 'first approximations, ignoring friction and air resistance', this indicates an important difference between idealization in science and logic or philosophy. Insofar as the aim of philosophy is to solve particular problems and to clarify specific unclarities and confusions, as the later Wittgenstein maintains, logical/philosophical models aren't idealized approximations to a proper account, contrary to how one might characterize scientific idealizations, such as leaving out friction from an account of free fall. Insofar as science aims to ultimately produce a non-idealized account, its ideal models may be regarded as mere approximations to a proper explanation offered later that takes into account all factors. By contrast, logical clarifications by means of idealized models can't be mere approximations. An approximation wouldn't account for everything needed to clarify the issue or to solve the problem. Consequently, 'complete clarity' couldn't be reached, contrary to Wittgenstein's stated aim (PI §133).

A crucial point here is that, whilst it might make sense in science to aim to complete an account so that it ultimately accounts for things as they really are in their actual complexity (for example, how air resistance and other factors affect falling objects), in logic and philosophy there's no corresponding abstract overall criterion for the completeness of an account. There's no abstract general criterion for what features of language use must be accounted for by a clarification, but this depends on what exactly the unclarity or problem is. More specifically, as new philosophical problems may always be raised about particular issues or concepts, there's no principled stopping point where we could say that all the problems have been solved and the account is therefore complete. Rather, a clarification is complete when it clarifies the particular unclarities it was intended to clarify and, if it does so, it isn't a mere approximation to a proper account. Thus, it's only in relation to particular clarificatory tasks that it makes sense to try to reach complete clarity which would make the problems in question 'completely disappear' (Z §440; PI §133).

2.2 Logical Models and Logical Necessity

As the preceding indicates, the criterion of correctness for later Wittgenstein's clarifications of language use by means of language-games, grammatical rules, and other clarificatory models, including logical calculi, isn't empirical accuracy. Empirical accuracy wouldn't be consistent with the possibility of idealization as described in the previous section since presenting language use as more simple, exact, or neat than it actually is would compromise empirical accuracy (cf. PI §77). As explained, however, Wittgensteinian descriptions serve the purpose of logical/grammatical clarification of unclarities and confusions relating to particular philosophical problems. Thus, whether a clarification is correct depends on whether it enables one to reach clarity about relevant logical or conceptual issues and to solve the problems, rather than on empirical accuracy. (This doesn't mean that descriptions that enable one to reach conceptual clarity bear no relation to empirically accurate descriptions. But the former are not reducible to the latter.) Continuously with the *Tractatus*, Wittgenstein therefore seems to keep regarding the disappearance of problems as the criterion of correctness for logical and philosophical accounts (PI §133, quoted above). However, an underlying, more general question, not fully answered by the preceding considerations, is whether Wittgenstein's later methods can really be regarded as methods of logic. This isn't possible, if his methods are methods of empirical description of language use, because, as explained, 1) this would make it impossible to meet the ideals of rigour of logic, that is, simplicity and exactness. But also because 2) this would make it impossible to account for exceptionless or universal logical necessity which can't be reduced to empirical generality.[22] However, Wittgenstein is as aware of this second issue as the first one, and he has an answer:

> What you say seems to amount to saying that logic belongs to the natural history of humans and that is not compatible with the hardness of the logical 'must'.
>
> But the logical 'must' is an element of the sentences of logic and these are not sentences of human natural history. (RFM VI §49/MS 164: 149–150; cf. PI §§241–242)

The problem Wittgenstein comments on can be described as follows. If logic is part of human natural history, something that has evolved together with humans

---

[22] When Russell later disparagingly describes Wittgenstein's later philosophy as 'idle tea table amusement' and 'slight help to lexicographers', he seems to assume that Wittgenstein is merely giving empirical descriptions of language use. He's right that this would call into question their logical and philosophical relevance (Russell 1959: 216–17).

as thinking and language-using animals, and if there's no underlying level of strict and neat crystalline rules or sublime logical structures, pure from the messiness of the empirical world, that can be appealed to in order to explain exceptionless logical necessity, how can its exceptionless or universal character be explained? Evidently, logical necessity can't be explained in terms of empirical regularities or generalities relating to language and thought because such regularities/generalities allow for exceptions. They aren't, in this sense, 'compatible with the hardness of the logical must'.[23] But then how is logical necessity explained?

It's crucial for answering this question that Wittgensteinian grammatical or logical statements aren't used to make empirical statements about language use. Rather, as explained, they constitute modes of representation or models that actual use is compared with in order to clarify its specific aspects. In this view, the proper expression for exceptionless logical necessity isn't assertions, propositions, or theses about actual language use. Rather, exceptionless necessity is to be conceived as a feature of logical models, for example of statements of grammatical rules, such as 'An 'inner process' stands in need of outward criteria' (PI §580). Notably, even though there evidently are inner processes whose presence isn't connected with external (bodily or behavioural) criteria,[24] this clarificatory rule expresses no restrictions to its generality. These considerations explain the sense in which the 'logical "must" is an element of the propositions of logic'. Exceptionless generality and necessity are features of logical/grammatical statements or models. As Wittgenstein also remarks: '*Essence* is expressed in grammar' (PI §371). The way to express that which is essential or necessary is by means of grammatical rules and other clarificatory models, as encoded into their structure, not by means of true/false propositions. In this regard Wittgenstein's later philosophy of logic is then importantly continuous with the *Tractatus*' view that the proper way to express logical necessity is to encode it into the structure of a logical notation.

In the *Investigations* Wittgenstein clarifies the difference between logical and empirical descriptions as follows. As he notes, that linguistic communication involves 'not only agreement in definitions, but also (odd as this may sound)

---

[23] Hardness here is a metaphor for logical and mathematical necessities seemingly being not subject to the change and corrosion that affect the empirical world. Whilst mountains will eventually crumble, 2+2 will equal 4 and not any less, regardless of the passage of time.

[24] An example is feeling unity with nature after a sauna, sitting outside on a quiet summer night. Whilst I am certain that many Finns know this feeling, there's no external expression for it that would distinguish it from simply sitting in silence after a sauna. Misconstruing Wittgenstein's remark as an exceptionless thesis, Kripke voices the obvious objection that this thesis seems to be empirically false; that is, there are counter-examples to it (Kripke 1982: 102–103). Insofar as Wittgenstein's rule is a clarificatory model to be used as an object of comparison, however, this objection misses its target.

agreement in judgments' 'seems to abolish logic' (PI §242).[25] This seems to abolish logic, because the agreement in judgements that upholds agreement in definitions is merely an empirical regularity in linguistic behaviour. If there's no underlying necessary a priori structure to language that logic is concerned with, such as the *Tractatus* postulated, and logic merely describes such empirical regularities of linguistic behaviour, logic seems indeed to have been abolished. However, as Wittgenstein remarks, commenting on this, although 'what we call "measuring" is in part determined by a certain constancy in the results of measurement', 'It is one thing to describe methods of measurement, and another to obtain and state results of measurement' (PI §242). The task of logic is comparable to the former. Logic clarifies concepts and conceptual relations, or the grammar of language use, not by making empirical statements but by articulating models whose purpose is to clarify whatever might be regarded as essential to the practices of language use. In this sense, to describe a method of measurement, for example, is to describe what one must do to obtain a correct result of measurement or to qualify as measuring at all. Such a description, we might say, spells out the principles that govern measuring from which one can't deviate and still qualify as measuring. The role of statements of logic is comparable to such statements about the methodology of measurement. Although the practices of measuring can be studied historically or anthropologically, this isn't the function of statements about its methodology, as illustrated by the fact that, unlike empirical descriptions of measuring practices, statements about the methodology of measuring are not falsified by the fact that people deviate from them. This just means that whatever these people do, it's not measuring.

A logical or grammatical investigation is thus concerned with articulating what is logically necessary and possible, as further exemplified by the discussions in the *Investigations* of whether certain kinds of mental occurrences are necessary for a person to qualify as following a rule and whether the use of the word 'pain' could be based on a private definition that only the speaker knows (cf. PI §§138ff., 243ff. respectively). Although these clarifications relate to empirically given phenomena, they seek to clarify their essential or necessary, not merely contingent, features. As Wittgenstein also explains, 'our investigation is directed not towards *phenomena*, but rather, as one might say, towards the "*possibilities*" of phenomena. What that means is that we call to mind the *kinds of statement* that we make about phenomena' (PI §91). With this purpose he

---

[25] Wittgenstein's point is that, unless we agreed on an overwhelming number of judgements, especially simple ones, such as the object next to me on the desk is a book, linguistic communication would not be possible. It rests in this sense on agreement in linguistic behaviour, which in turn is reliant also on the constancy of other facts of nature (see Section 3).

then asks, for example, 'Is what we call "following a rule" something that it would be possible for only *one* person, only *once* in a lifetime, to do?', immediately clarifying the sense of the question, 'And this is, of course, a gloss on the *grammar* of the expression "to follow a rule"' (PI §199). His answer to this question is no; rule-following is a custom or a practice (PI §§199, 202). Note that, if rule-following, by contrast, were a mental state or a process, it could indeed conceivably occur only once in the life of just one person. This illustrates how calling to mind the kinds of statements we make can clarify the logic or grammar of our concepts or what is logically necessary or possible.[26]

The discontinuity between Wittgenstein's early and later philosophy with regard to these issues then relates to his later account of the employment of models as objects of comparison. As explained, this is intended as a solution to the problem of the sublimation of logic, misleading simplifications and generalizations, dogmatism, and relapse to metaphysical theses, which negatively affected the *Tractatus*. By contrast, in Wittgenstein's later philosophy the acknowledgement of exceptions and further complexities of language use is made possible by distinguishing clearly between models and what they are models of, and by paying attention to *both* the similarities and differences between actual language use and models thereof. This not only puts one in a position to acknowledge the ways in which actual reality differs from the models used to describe it. It's also important for understanding Wittgenstein's method that a mode of representation that provides an orderly view of certain regularities of language use can help to perceive perspicuously exceptions from those regularities too. Clarificatory definitions/rules or idealized cases can in this sense be used as what Wittgenstein calls 'centres of variation', whereby features of actual cases, including mixed cases that exhibit characteristics of more than one definition or idealized case, can be clarified by envisaging them as variations from our clarificatory definitions and cases which, for purposes of clarification, are regarded as central (see MS 115: 221–222; cf. MS 152: 16–17). (Asserting that certain cases are *the* central ones would again mean relapsing to a substantial thesis.)

We have now reached a point where it's possible to comment on different interpretations of the later Wittgenstein regarding the dis/continuity of his philosophy. A key issue here is whether Wittgenstein's language-games and grammatical rules ought to be understood as means of clarification or the target of clarification. Are grammatical rules and language-games modes of

---

[26] For the difference between logical or grammatical and empirical statements, see also below Wittgenstein's remarks on the non-temporal use of grammatical statements, and Section 3.3 for how the generality and justification of grammatical statements differs from that of empirical statements.

describing language use (and instruments of description in this sense) or are they the object or target of Wittgensteinian descriptions? Whilst in the preceding I adopted the former point of view, the issue is controversial. (A main representative of the latter view is Peter Hacker who in his various writings takes the goal of Wittgenstein's clarifications to be rendering perspicuous the *rules* of language, instead of regarding grammatical rules as modes of describing language with the goal of rendering perspicuous its *uses*.) Although this isn't the place to try to solve this dispute, it's important to observe the questions that arise for the interpretations that regard language-games and grammatical rules as the target rather than a means of clarification.[27] How do they avoid a relapse to true/false claims or theses about grammar or logic, or about actual language use, analogous to those of the *Tractatus*? How are the problems relating to dogmatism, idealization, and the sublimation of logic avoided? Relatedly, such interpretations need to explain what Wittgenstein means by saying that language-games are objects of comparison (PI §130), and what the logical status of grammatical statements is. Problematically, regarded as statements about rules that actually govern language use, grammatical statements seem to constitute either empirical assertions about language or logical or metaphysical theses about necessities pertaining to its use. Neither of these accounts fits well with what Wittgenstein says.

With regard to these issues it's instructive to consider a remark from the early 1930s that reveals how Wittgenstein contrasts grammatical rules with empirical assertions about actual language use:

> What I am calling a 'rule' must not contain anything about a particular (or even general) time or place for its application, and must not refer to particular people (or people in general); it only constitutes an instrument of representation.
>
> We say: 'We use the words "red" and "green" in such a way that it is considered senseless (is contradictory) to say that there is red and green in the same place at the same time'. And of course this is a proposition, an empirical proposition, about our actual language. (MS 113: 29v/TS 212: 716/TS 213: 246r/BT, 193)

---

[27] Kuusela 2008 and 2019c argue for the interpretation of grammatical rules as instruments of clarification. It's important to note, however, that this view doesn't exclude the possibility of talking about uses of language in terms of grammatical rules and language-games. Rather, the point is exactly that, when speaking of language from the perspective of Wittgenstein's methods, we can ask questions such as, 'what rules are the use of this expression governed by?' or 'what language-games do we play with this expression?' Such questions aren't answered by means of theses about the rules that actually govern language use, however, but by articulating clarificatory models that enable us to make sense of the use of relevant expressions.

This captures the crux of Wittgenstein's distinction between temporal and non-temporal statements that he uses to explain the role of grammatical, logical, and mathematical statements in contrast to empirical statements and to clarify the exceptionless/universal character of statements about logical and mathematical necessity (see also MS 117: 24; MS 117: 25/MS 118: 18r; TS 221: 156–157; RFM I §102). Whilst a temporal statement involves (an explicit or implicit) reference to a time and place, which may be particular or general, non-temporal statements don't refer to any time(s) or place(s). That logical or grammatical statements involve no reference to time and place then explains their exceptionless generality or universality. Such a statement is exceptionless, because it doesn't refer to any actual instances of use, either individually or generally, to begin with. Moreover, unlike an exceptionless metaphysical thesis, a grammatical statement is non-substantial in that it isn't a generalization regarding all cases either.[28] As Wittgenstein says, it constitutes a mode of representing relevant cases. In this sense it's an instrument of description.

It's then crucial that, in order to say anything about actual language use, a non-temporal statement has to be brought into contact with actual use by comparing actual use with it. This puts us in a position to fully understand the point of Wittgenstein's characterization of the use and logical status of clarificatory models as objects of comparison. This characterization provides us with a third way to understand the function of logical or philosophical models, besides the alternatives of using such models to make empirical claims about actual language use or using them to make metaphysical claims about necessities pertaining to language use. Clarifications in terms of models used as objects of comparison constitute neither kind of claims/theses. They are not empirical assertions about particular cases or inductive generalizations over them but neither are they exceptionless/universal philosophical theses arrived at through abstraction. Crucially, if we project the exceptionless/universal necessity expressed by a logical/grammatical statement onto language in the form of a claim about a necessity governing actual language use, we are putting forward a thesis about language similar to that made in the *Tractatus*. In so doing we have again run together the mode and the object of representation, representing the former as capturing the essence of the latter.

This, then, is the problem with interpretations that regard grammatical rules and language-games as the object rather than the means of description. They risk turning grammatical statements into substantial theses about

---

[28] A metaphysical generalization through abstraction, just like an empirical inductive generalization over cases, is still substantial, as Wittgenstein notes in the pre-Tractarian *Notebooks* about Russell's propositional functions where all terms have been turned into variables (NB: 17/MS 101: 58r).

language use and, to the extent that they do so, they fail to move beyond the *Tractatus'* unsuccessful attempt to abandon theses. Consequently, they risk repeating its 'grave mistakes' in a new form by projecting the later Wittgenstein's modes of representing language use onto actual language. Here they fall again for the illusion of predicating of the thing what lies in the mode of representing it (PI §104). For it's an illusion, comparable to the optical illusions of misidentifying the colour of an object because one is wearing tinted glasses, to conflate a necessary, constitutive, or characteristic feature of the philosopher's mode of representation with a necessary, constitutive, or characteristic feature of the object of representation (MS 157a: 57v–58r; MS 157b: 3v, 9v). In Wittgenstein's account exceptionless/universal logical necessity isn't a peculiar feature of reality that has to be accessed through philosophical abstraction or by reaching in some other way beyond the impure and messy empirical reality. Rather, as he says, exceptionless/universal logical necessity is an 'element of the sentences of logic'. In this way his later philosophy of logic sheds the metaphysical trappings of logic. In logic we don't speak about or refer to peculiar non-temporal objects and structures, but we employ the statements of logic non-temporally. The reality we speak about in logic is the old messy reality, not an ideal reality. But when we speak about this messy reality we may need to idealize and abstract away some of its features in order to highlight what is relevant to the task of logical clarification.[29]

3 Later Wittgenstein's New Logical Methods

According to the later Wittgenstein, the problems of philosophy, and therefore the methods needed to address them, are logical (LW I, §256, quoted in the introduction). However, there are many such methods, and Wittgenstein emphasizes the need to choose the right ones for specific clarificatory tasks (PI §133;

---

[29] Although their positions might appear similar, it's a mistake to confuse Wittgenstein's view with Carnap's conventionalism. Whilst both agree that the right way to express logical necessity is a statement of a rule, not substantial metaphysical theses, Wittgenstein isn't committed to Carnap's thesis about conventions as the *source* of necessity. The source of necessity might also be something in nature. For example, the exclusion of reddish-green may have to do with features of the human brain where groups of cells are set up so as to enhance the red-green contrast. Whatever the source of necessity might be, however, the necessity is properly expressed by a grammatical rule, not statements about empirical regularities (see Kuusela 2008: chapter 5 for discussion). Here it's then important that hypotheses about the brain or whatever might be the source of the perceived regularity, understood in the sense of empirical explanations of why we have the concepts we have or why we draw the distinctions that we do, aren't relevant for grammatical/logical clarification. The point of grammatical investigation is to clarify our concepts, not to explain why we have the concepts we have (see Section 3.3). And of course, empirical facts about the brain could not justify exceptionless logical/grammatical statements.

RC §§43–46, quoted in the introduction). This section provides an overview of Wittgenstein's novel logical methods. Having explained in Section 2 how his later methods can be understood as methods of logic rather than empirical inquiry, I will now assume this. But in Section 3.3 I will comment on certain formal differences between empirical statements and logical/grammatical statements relating to their generality and justification that further clarify the difference between logical and empirical statements.

On the interpretation adopted in this Element, the later Wittgenstein doesn't reject calculus-based logical methods as methods of logical and philosophical clarification. Such methods have their own areas of application and may be useful especially in connection with mathematics: a calculus according to definite rules is a good way to clarify the features of another similar calculus (cf. AWL: 138). Nevertheless, Wittgenstein came to regard calculus-based methods as having only a limited use in philosophy, because in philosophy we often deal with highly complex concepts originating in colloquial language, such as meaning, truth, goodness, and freedom, that are difficult if not impossible to clarify in terms of the simple and exact rules of a calculus. Another problem is that the methods of Fregean–Russellian–Tractarian logic are still too much focused on grammatical form instead of the use of language, even though an explicit motive for both Frege and Russell was to use logic to go beyond mere surface grammar and its psychological distinctions, and to clarify the logical forms of relevant expressions. This problem is exemplified by the failure of truth-functional logic to recognize statements such as 'It is raining but I don't believe it' (an instance of what is known as Moore's paradox) as contradictions, given that here there's no formal contradiction in the sense of p and $\neg$p, and logic focused on grammatical forms can't recognize the sameness of the use of 'I believe it is raining' and 'It is raining' in relevant contexts. Wittgenstein comments on this:

> This shows serious gaps in logic. It indicates – what so many things indicate – that what we usually call 'logic' is only applicable to a tiny part of the game with language. This is also why logic is as uninteresting as, judging by its appearance, it should be interesting. (MS 132: 119–120)

It's plausible that the methods introduced by the later Wittgenstein are intended to fill in these kinds of gaps in logic. Insofar as his new methods succeed in doing so, they can be understood as extending logic to areas where calculus-based methods cease to be useful. Thus, calculus-based methods emerge as a special case of logical methodology. Besides them logical methods also include: a) the method of language-games, which consists of clarifying the use/role of words as part of activities and human life by means of simple language-games employed as models, b) the description of language use by stating grammatical rules, and c) Wittgensteinian natural history or quasi-ethnology, which consists of the use of real or fictional natural history to clarify the dependencies of language use on psychological and physical facts about speakers and their environment. Each method involves the employment of models as objects of comparison, in the sense of Section 2, or more broadly as instruments of clarification, as outlined below. As will become evident, these methods are connected through overlapping similarities and form a family in the sense of cases falling under family-resemblance concepts. (For family-resemblance, see Section 4.2.) The set of methods is therefore open-ended and extensible rather than closed.

3.1 The Method of Language-Games

Wittgenstein says in his lectures that 'Language-games are a clue to the understanding of logic' (AWL: 12). The point is that, whilst Frege and Russell, and the *Tractatus* following them, assumed that a general definition of the notion of thought or proposition should constitute the foundation or core of a system of logic (cf. Section 1), the notion of a proposition covers many different uses of words, for example empirical and mathematical propositions.[30] There isn't just one calculus of propositions and neither Frege's, nor Russell's, nor the *Tractatus*' calculus can be regarded as *the* fundamental one (AWL: 13). As Wittgenstein comments on his early view: 'I had the mistaken idea that propositions only belong to just one calculus. There seemed to be one funda-mental calculus, viz., logic, on which any other calculus could be based' (AWL: 138). Instead, he now proposes to build logic around the notion of a language-game that can accommodate a variety of different uses of language, including different kinds of propositions and calculi, without giving priority to any in particular and without any commitment to reductively explain all the possible uses of language in terms of some specific kind of use, such as the Tractarian propositions and truth-functions built out of them (cf. PI §23). Thus, with the notion of language-game we can avoid relying on any preconceived ideas about the function of language and the misleading simplifications they might bring along.

---

[30] Within these classes we can further distinguish between different uses of relevant expressions, as Wittgenstein first had to acknowledge in the case of colour words whose use doesn't conform to Tractarian truth-functions (RLF). Another example of the variety of uses is the descriptions of mental states, some of which build on expressive uses of words whilst others employ words with already extant use in 'secondary sense' (PI §244, PPF §§275–278. See Section 4.3 for the notion of secondary sense).

When introducing language-games in the *Investigations* Wittgenstein characterizes them as follows: 'I shall ... call the whole, consisting of language and the actions into which it is woven, the "language-game"' (PI §7); 'to imagine a language is to imagine a form of life' (PI §19); 'the term "language-game" is meant to bring into prominence the fact that the speaking of language is part of an activity, or of a form of life' (PI §23). The idea is that the uses of language are embedded in actions and forms of behaviour of linguistic agents in the surroundings of their life. Consequently, if we want to understand the logical/grammatical function of our words, we need to examine the role they play as part of human activities and life. As Wittgenstein remarks about the concept of pain: 'The concept of pain is characterized through a specific function in our life' (TS 233b: 32). And:

> The concept of pain is embedded in our life in a certain way. It is characterized by very definite connexions. ...
>
> Only surrounded by certain normal manifestations of life is there such a thing as an expression of pain. (TS 232: 640; cf. MS 136, 28b–29a; TS 233b: 32/Z §§532–534)

Hence, we can say more generally: 'To describe a language-game is to describe the actions of human beings' (MS 119: 147r; cf. 148r).

The method of language-games, therefore, can be characterized as a method for studying the functioning of linguistic expressions in the context of the activities and life of which they are part. However, such contexts may be extremely complex and it may be difficult to achieve a perspicuous view of them. Consequently, the idea of language use as part of a form of life and embedded in activities can't by itself explain how the task of clarification is carried out.[31] In order to explain how language-games help to deal with complex and fluctuating uses of colloquial language, we need to take note of another feature of language-games, that is, their simplicity or primitivity. As Wittgenstein explains: '[Language-games] are ways of using signs simpler than those in which we use the signs of our highly complicated everyday language. ... The study of language games is the study of primitive forms of language or primitive languages' (BB: 17; my square brackets; cf. PI §§5, 7). The point is that, with the help of simple language-games employed as models, one can bring into focus specific aspects or facets of complicated uses of language. Thus one can abstract from and take apart complicated uses of linguistic expressions with the purpose of clarifying their different aspects

---

[31] This is sometimes ignored by Wittgensteinians who speak of language-games in very general terms, such as the language-game of religion, but in so doing arguably reduce the method of language-games to mere hand waving. See Hilmy 1987: 184ff. for a criticism along these lines.

and analysing them in this sense (cf. PI §90). This enables one to cut through the complexities of actual language use and to achieve a perspicuous view of its uses. As Wittgenstein writes in the *Investigations*, explaining the purpose of the very first language-game introduced there, the so-called shopping or grocery language-game: 'It disperses the fog [created by the general concept of meaning] if we study the phenomena of language in primitive kinds of use in which one can clearly survey the purpose and functioning of the words' (PI §5; my square brackets). The point is that thinking about the function of words in general terms, such as 'having meaning', 'signifying', 'referring', or 'naming', is apt to cover up what we need to attend to in order to understand the different kinds of uses words have (cf. PI §§10, 17). Accordingly, Wittgenstein gives the following general characterization of the point of language-games:

> If we want to study the problems of truth and falsehood, of the agreement and disagreement of propositions with reality, of the nature of assertion, assumption, and question, we shall with great advantage look at primitive forms of language in which these forms of thinking appear without the confusing background of highly complicated processes of thought. When we look at such simple forms of language the mental mist which seems to enshroud our ordinary use of language disappears. We see activities, reactions, which are clear-cut and transparent. On the other hand we recognize in these simple processes forms of language not separated by a break from our more complicated ones. We see that we can build up the complicated forms from the primitive ones by gradually adding new forms. (BB: 17)

The shopping/grocery language-game at the start of the *Investigations* can be used to illustrate how language-games work, for example how they can be used to draw attention to differences in the use of words.[32] Notably, in order to clarify such differences, language-games don't need to be realistic or empirically accurate, just as the shopping/grocery game isn't. (No one shops for apples as described in language-game §1, including Cantabrigians in the 1930s.) Rather, to bring out relevant differences it may help to exaggerate the features characteristic of different uses similarly to caricatures, as Wittgenstein can be understood to be doing in *Investigations* §1 by connecting the use of names with the use of name tags and the use of colour words with the colour samples. For, although we do sometimes use colour samples to explain which colour is spoken

---

[32] The shopping/grocery language-game distinguishes between three different uses: the referring use of names, the use of numerals for counting by correlating objects with them, and the use of colour words with reference to samples of relevant colours (PI §1). As the example shows, the use of each word kind is quite different from the others. Such differences are apt to disappear from view, however, if we speak of the issue in general terms such as having meaning, or if we try to explain all the mentioned uses in terms of referring to objects. (Referring is a particular mode of use, not something to which all uses can be reduced.)

of when getting colours exactly right is important, it's an exaggeration that we would use them to distinguish between red, green, and yellow apples. Neither do we usually tag objects to identify them, as the shopkeeper does, keeping apples in a drawer marked with the name 'apples'. Nevertheless, these exaggerations help to highlight differences in the use of relevant words.

From such simple uses we can then build up more complicated ones, as Wittgenstein says in the last quotation from the *Blue Book*, whilst retaining the perspicuity of our descriptions by only adding complexity gradually. As he explains: 'The advantage of the examination of language-games is just that they let us see *gradually* what otherwise we only see as a *whole*, and that is, as a tangled clew' (TS 228: 177; cf. MS 162b: 52v, 53r). As this indicates, language-games lose their clarificatory capacity relative to an increase in their complexity, unless complexity is built up gradually. Hence, the simplicity of language-games employed as models is indeed crucial to the method of language-games. Another important point is that when building more complex games out of simpler ones, the goal isn't to develop out of simple language-games a theory of how language actually functions, as if they were 'first approximations, ignoring friction and air resistance' (PI §130, quoted in Section 2). This, as Wittgenstein explains in an early version of PI §§130–131, would risk doing injustice to the complexities of actual language use, and constitute a relapse to dogmatic theses:

> When I describe certain simple language games, this is not in order to describe on their basis the processes of our actual developed language, which would only lead to injustices. (Nicod & Russell.) Rather, we let the language-games be what they are. They should only emanate their clarifying effect on our problems. (MS 115: 81)

Relatedly, Wittgenstein responds to the objection that his descriptions of language-games don't cover all uses of relevant words: 'the simple language-games play a quite different role. They are poles of a description, not the ground-floor of a theory' (RPP I §633/TS 229: 334/TS 245: 246). This is connected with the point that the purpose of language-games isn't to describe the actual uses of words in their full complexity. Evidently, we do much more with numbers than the shopkeeper in the grocery/shopping language-game, for example. (For all we know, he can't even add numbers. From Wittgenstein's point of view we can see addition as constituting a further facet of the use of number words besides their use to count by correlating objects with them.) Rather, language-games are poles of description in the sense that, used as models, they enable one to focus on specific aspects of use and then study those uses in isolation or in relation to one another, for example in order to clarify how certain uses build on others. Consequently, language-games also put one in a position to clarify how complex concepts are constituted by different kinds of uses of relevant words, as exemplified by number words or psychological concepts, with the latter typically having both descriptive and expressive uses, neither of which is reducible to the other. As illustrated by the concepts of seeing and pain, both of which have first-person expressive and descriptive uses as well as third-person descriptive uses, it isn't possible to make sense of these concepts unless we account for the different facets of the use of relevant words that together make up the concept (RPP I §63).[33] The point about language-games as poles of description, not a full-blown theory or a starting point for a theory, is connected with the point in Section 2 that what is important for logical clarification is that anything relevant for the particular clarificatory task at hand is taken into account. As noted, the latter constitutes the criterion for the completeness of clarificatory descriptions of language use.

However, it's important to notice that not all uses of language-games are descriptive in the sense just outlined. Language-games can be used for logical clarification in other ways too. Thus, in the *Investigations* Wittgenstein makes use of simple language-games, for example to clarify the notion of rule-following: 'Let us now examine the following kind of language-game: when A gives an order B has to write down series of signs according to a certain formation rule' (PI §143). Whilst this evidently is a simple language-game employed for the purpose of clarification, its function isn't to describe the use of the notion of rule-following or any particular aspect of it. Rather, the language-game provides us with a simple case in the context of which we can examine what rule-following involves, which then enables us to clarify the related, more nebulous concepts of meaning and understanding a rule in a certain way. By contrast, if one simply asks what it is to mean or understand a word in a certain way, the temptation may be overwhelming to explain this in terms of a mental state that fixes the meaning of the word. As Wittgenstein's example makes clear,

---

[33] If I exclaim, 'I see a fox!' and you describe me by saying, 'He sees a fox', it's crucial that we are speaking of one and the same state of seeing, despite the fact that my use is an expressive first-person use and yours a descriptive true/false third-person use. If this unity of the concept is broken, it will no longer make sense, for example, to ask another to confirm what one sees. In just this way the misconstrual of seeing as a private mental state that is not accessible to others excludes the possibility of the epistemic practice of asking others to confirm what one sees, thus creating a conflict between our actual linguistic practices and philosophical accounts thereof, which gives rise to philosophical problems, that is, anomalies that constitute a reason for saying the account doesn't 'add up' (cf. RPP I §§548–549/TS 229: 314; cf. TLP 4.1213). Another example of difficulties that arise from misdescribing the uses of psychological terms is David Chalmers's argument about the 'hard problem of consciousness' which involves a failure to consider the different aspects of the use of psychological expressions, focusing narrowly on third-person use only. Due to this, his argument fails to establish the existence of the 'hard problem' (see Kuusela 2016).

however, in the case of writing down a mathematical series the state of mind would have to fix an infinite number of steps of how the series is meant to be continued. Thus, it would have to achieve what no physical mechanism seems able to do (PI §188). Further, as the example also helps to clarify, mental occurrences, such as having a mathematical formula in mind, are in principle open to various interpretations, just as any formula written on paper. This indicates a further problem with mentalistic explanations of meaning and understanding (PI §140).

Although the preceding is merely a sketch, I hope it makes clear how the method of language-games makes possible the clarification of complicated and fluctuating uses of natural language whose dynamic character and complexity make it very difficult or impossible to present them in terms of the fixed and precise rules of a calculus. Indeed, it's difficult to see how a Fregean–Russellian logical calculus could be used to analyse the different uses of words that make up, for example, our psychological concepts, given the focus of the calculus on the logical functions of subsuming objects under names, predication (including many placed predicates or relations), and quantification. At the same time, just like logical calculi, the method of language-games makes use of abstraction and idealization as ways to achieve clarity. A basic insight behind language-games in this regard is that a simple description of something complex can be rectified by narrowing its scope (PI §3). This explains how otherwise misleadingly simplistic logical or philosophical accounts, such as Augustine's picture of language as consisting of only names, can contribute to logical/grammatical clarification. (Rather than being put forward as theses, such modes of representation are better understood as models to be used as objects of comparison which then allow one to recognize and acknowledge the complexity of actual uses and to render the simplification harmless.) Additionally, Wittgenstein makes use of the idea of gradually building complexity into models, which helps to retain perspicuity in the case of complex logical structures. This highlights the processual character of logical/philosophical clarification.

3.2 The Method of Grammatical Rules

As illustrated by the next quotation, the methods of language-games and grammatical rules overlap; their boundaries aren't clear cut. On the one hand, insofar as the language-game method consists of envisaging language as a game according to rules, it overlaps with the method of describing uses of language by means of rules. On the other hand, as the quotations in the previous section show, the method of language-games doesn't involve any commitment to speaking about language in terms of rules. No mention of rules is made when

Wittgenstein first introduces language-games in the *Investigations*; language-games are merely described as involving the embeddedness of language in actions and forms of life. The overlap between these two methods is evident in the following remark, which also makes clear that descriptions of language use in terms of rules involve abstraction and idealization in the sense explained in Section 2.

> If we look at the actual use of a word, what we see is something constantly fluctuating.
>
> In our investigations we set over against this fluctuation something more fixed, just as one paints a stationary picture of the constantly altering face of the landscape.
>
> When we study language we *envisage* it as a game with fixed rules. We compare it with, and measure it against, a game of that kind.
>
> If for our purposes we wish to regulate the use of a word by definite rules, then alongside its fluctuating use we set up a different use by codifying one of its characteristic aspects.
>
> Thus it could be said that the use of the word "good" (in an ethical sense) is a combination of a very large number of interrelated games, each of them as it were a facet of the use. What makes a single concept here is precisely the connection, the relationship, between these facets. (PG: 77/MS 140: 33–34)

The description of language use in terms of rules thus only involves comparing language with a game according to rules or envisaging it as such a game. No claim is made about language use being a necessarily rule-governed activity. Indeed, Wittgenstein explicitly rejects the latter claim as false: 'we do not actually assert that language is a game which is played according to rules (for otherwise we are asserting something false), but we compare the phenomena of language with such a game, and the one is more or less similar to the other' (VW: 35/MS 302: 14; cf. PI §§81–83, AWL: 47–48). Moreover, as the quotation from *Philosophical Grammar* says, descriptions of language use in terms of rules constitute idealizations in that they present something fluctuating and dynamic in a static and definite way, like a painting of a landscape has to freeze the landscape and try to capture something characteristic of it.

As such, the method of grammatical rules is straightforward to describe. It involves the description of the uses of language in terms of rules or systems thereof, as exemplified by 'the meaning of a word is its use in the language' (PI §43; cf. PG: 59–60/MS 140: 15r, which offers a 'mini-system' of relevant rules). Here, the rules in terms of which language is described figure as modes of representing language use or as models to be employed as objects of comparison. (As explained in Section 2, the exceptionless necessity expressed by a rule is to be understood as a feature of the model. This necessity isn't to be projected onto language as a thesis about a necessity found in actual language use.) Accordingly, the main difference between the methods of grammatical rules and language-games is that descriptions in terms of rules don't involve descriptions of actions in the sense of, for example, Wittgenstein's shopping/ grocery game in *Investigations* §1. Consequently, descriptions in terms of rules may be more abstract, apt for highlighting general regularities in language use or similarities between the uses of different expressions, as exemplified by *Investigations* §580 (quoted in Section 2.2). For although Wittgenstein is critical of what he calls 'craving for generality' in philosophy (BB: 18), this doesn't mean that observing general regularities in the use of words wouldn't be important for logical/philosophical clarification. An example of such a generality, connected with the point in §580 that inner states require external criteria, is the pattern that psychological verbs typically have both expressive first-person uses and descriptive third-person uses.

To connect this method with more traditional philosophical methodology, the method of grammatical rules can be seen as a modification of the philosophical practice of stating definitions for concepts or whatever they speak about. (A definition provides a rule for the use of a word as the expression of a certain concept.) Wittgenstein's modification to this practice is that for him there's no such thing as *the* ultimate definition, such as Socrates is described as looking for in the Platonic dialogues. Rather, from Wittgenstein's point of view we can recognize a wider range of uses for rules as instruments of clarification, including the definition of simplified notions that serve the discussion of particular problems, and aren't meant to account for all cases falling under relevant concepts.[34]

Another important difference relates to the philosophical tradition's construction of definitions as true/false theses. By contrast, Wittgensteinian grammatical rules aren't employed as true/false theses/propositions but as objects of comparison. Consequently, this approach makes it possible to use multiple rules to simultaneously characterize different aspects of the use of a word. Importantly, because grammatical rules don't constitute true/false theses, they don't exclude other rules in the way in which incompatible true theses/propositions do. Thus, Wittgenstein's approach makes possible what can be called 'multi-dimensional logical descriptions' (not his term) whereby different rules are employed simultaneously to clarify different aspects of a complex use of words (see

---

[34] It can be argued that Socrates himself uses definitions for a variety of purposes, such as ensuring the possibility of communication and collaboration, although this has been obscured by the philosophical tradition, following on from Plato, focused on finding the ultimate definition. Kuusela 2019d distinguishes several employments of definitions shared by the Socrates of the Platonic dialogues and Wittgenstein.

Kuusela 2019c: chapter 6.5). This is exemplified by saying that psychological verbs have both expressive and descriptive uses. (A statement such as 'in the third person the verb "see" is used descriptively' can be understood as stating a grammatical rule.) However, with regard to the employment of such rules for the purpose of logical or philosophical clarification, it's noteworthy that there are instances of the use of colloquial language where we don't or can't distinguish between such different uses but relevant expressions are used, so to speak, on the borderline of the two types of use. An example is 'I'm so scared', which in particular circumstances might be either an expression/manifestation of my fear or a description of my mental state, as when I confess my fear to you. However, the sentence can also be used in a way that makes it impossible to distinguish between the two uses. In such a case the two descriptions can be seen as centres of variation (cf. Section 2) around which the use of the sentence oscillates. Here the descriptions constitute poles of description in the sense explained earlier.

3.3 Natural History and Wittgensteinian Naturalism in Logic

As Wittgenstein observes, 'Commanding, questioning, recounting, chatting, are as much a part of our natural history as walking, eating, drinking, playing' (PI §25). Accordingly, there's a sense in which, by clarifying modes of language use, we are concerned with human natural history and humans as a certain kind of natural historical beings. As Wittgenstein also remarks: 'What we are supplying are really remarks on the natural history of human beings; not curiosities, however, but facts that no one has doubted, which have escaped notice only because they are always before our eyes' (PI §415). And: 'When I describe language, I describe the way people behave, so to speak, ethnologically' (MS 124: 253; cf. MS 162b: 67v/CV: 45; MS 117: 256). This doesn't mean understanding logical descriptions as empirical statements about human natural history. As noted in Section 2.2, this would make it impossible to explain exceptionless/ universal logical necessity because empirical generalities allow for exceptions. Such an account of logic would therefore not be compatible with 'the hardness of the logical must' (RFM VI §49; PI §§241–242). How this problem with empiricist naturalism is avoided will become clearer in due course.

Underlying Wittgenstein's concern with natural history is the idea fundamental to the method of language-games that language use is embedded in actions and the behaviour of humans, being part of a form of life in this sense. Consequently, modes of language use are influenced in various ways by human psychology and related human characteristics, such as their capacity to feel and express pain, which is unlearned and in this sense primitive and non-linguistic. However, modes of behaviour such as pain behaviour may also take a linguistic form, and in this capacity they can be regarded as extensions of non-linguistic modes of human behaviour. As Wittgenstein remarks: 'Believing that someone else is in pain, doubting whether he is, are so many natural kinds of behaviour towards other human beings; and our language is but an auxiliary to and extension of this behaviour. I mean: our language is an extension of the more primitive behaviour' (RPP I §151/TS 229: 225/TS 245: 160; cf. Z §545, MS 130: 206). Moreover, even in cases where there are no such underlying primitive, non-linguistic modes of behaviour, natural historical facts still influence language use in various ways. As Wittgenstein notes: 'Concepts with fixed limits would demand a uniformity of behaviour. But where I am certain, someone else is uncertain. And that is a fact of nature' (MS 137: 65b/TS 232: 764/TS 233b: 4/RPP II §683/Z §374).

Wittgensteinian naturalism isn't only concerned with the psychology of humans, however. More generally, it seeks to clarify the functioning of language from the perspective of embodied beings in interaction with their environment, as also suggested by the notion of form of life. (Life assumes particular forms in specific environments. Such forms can't be simply detached from their environments, even if they might be able to adjust to similar environments.) This is important in that some features of the use of words are only rendered comprehensible – as opposed to appearing arbitrary and perhaps defective – when examined in light of facts pertaining to the environment of language users, not only facts about language users. For example, Frege and Russell perceived the lack of exactness of colloquial language as a defect, whilst Wittgenstein's observation about the lack of uniformity of human behaviour seeks to make comprehensible the lack of clear and fixed conceptual limits. Wittgenstein writes about this dependence of linguistic practices on facts of nature:

> if things were quite different from what they actually are — if there were for instance no characteristic expression of pain, of fear, of joy; if rule became exception and exception rule; or if both became phenomena of roughly equal frequency – – this would make our normal language-games lose their point. – The procedure of putting a lump of cheese on a balance and fixing the price by the turn of the scale would lose its point if it frequently happened that such lumps suddenly grew or shrank with no obvious cause . . .. (PI §142)

Certain linguistic practices are only possible against the background of certain facts relating to humans and their environment. However, it's crucial for Wittgenstein's point of view that his natural historical approach isn't an attempt to explain in a scientific or quasi-scientific way why our modes of language use or conceptual formations are whatever they are.[35] Rather, the purpose is to describe and clarify features of language use in relation to facts about humans and their environment. Notably, this purpose can be equally served by fictional natural history, exemplified by Wittgenstein's discussions of various fictional tribes, or cases such as our using others as slaves that function as reading machines or calculators, and examples like the one just quoted about weighing cheese. (The imaginary case of cheeses growing and shrinking readily brings to view the dependence of our actual practices of certain natural regularities.) As this makes clear, Wittgenstein's goal isn't to explain language in terms of any facts about humans or their environment, but merely to describe and clarify. He comments on this:

> If the formation of concepts can be explained by facts of nature, should we not be interested, not in grammar, but rather in that in nature which is the basis of grammar? – Our interest certainly includes the correspondence between concepts and very general facts of nature. (Such facts as mostly do not strike us because of their generality.) But our interest doesn't fall back upon these possible causes of the formation of concepts; we are not doing natural science; nor yet natural history – since we can also invent fictitious natural history for our purposes. (PI II: 230/PPF §365)

An example of Wittgenstein's use of natural historical considerations for the purpose of logical clarification is *Investigations* §244 where he proposes an account of linguistic first-person pain expressions as an extension of non-linguistic pain behaviour. On this account, the linguistic expressions of pain replace its natural expressions, such as crying and moaning, whilst retaining a similar function. *Investigations* §244 thus describes the use of relevant expressions as partly determined and shaped by certain psychological and/or physical facts about human beings. In Wittgenstein's account, such facts relating to humans as bodily beings constitute the background for the use of linguistic expressions of pain, without which the latter couldn't get off the ground. For, as he argues in connection with his so-called private language argument, it isn't possible to understand talk about pain as founded on a private definition of what pain is by privately pointing to a relevant sensation and resolving to use certain expressions to refer to the same sensation in the future. (Names as a specific kind of linguistic expressions require criteria of correctness

---

[35] An example of a quasi-scientific philosophical explanation would be explaining rule-following in terms of the agreement of actions of rule-followers as a necessary condition of rule-following, as if we had a notion of the sameness of actions of rule-following independently of the notion of rule (cf. PI §§224–225). Instead Wittgenstein's point is merely descriptive: a characteristic of rule-following is that rule-followers agree on how a rule is followed (see Kuusela 2019c: 209–210).

for their use but a 'private definition' can at best provide a false appearance of there being such criteria, not anything against which one could independently check that one uses the expression consistently for the same sensation; PI §§263, 265, 268.) Thus, on Wittgenstein's account, having set up 'the connection between the name and the thing named' by teaching a child the expressive first-person use, whereby she replaces crying and moaning with linguistic expressions and the word 'pain' acquires a definite use and role in her life, further descriptive uses can be made of relevant words in the third and first person. For example, a parent might respond to a child asking where the pain is and the child in turn point at the sore spot and say where it hurts. (Not all first-person uses of sensation words are expressive. We can talk about our past pains or describe our current pains, for example.)

The philosophical gain here is that, equipped with such an alternative account of the function of relevant expressions, we can address the so-called problem of other minds; that is, the seeming impossibility of knowing the mental states of others, which arises from the problematic idea that the foundation of talk about mental states is the kind of private definitions that the private language argument problematizes. By contrast, Wittgenstein's account eliminates the traditionally presumed gap between the inner and the outer by introducing the notion of expressive behaviour. This can then be further developed to explain the possibility of knowledge of the sensations of others, for example seeing pain or sadness on the face of another (see Kuusela 2019c: 185ff.).

Investigations §244 can therefore be characterized as describing an aspect of language use by means of a natural historical picture or a natural historical model. Were this intended as an empirical claim, it should be backed up with evidence, but any such evidence is conspicuously absent from Wittgenstein's discussion. Indeed, he explicitly qualifies his account with, 'Here is one possibility' (PI §244). This is important in that presenting such an alternative possibility is all that he needs to question the traditional philosophical picture of sensation talk as based on private definitions – or almost all. For it's also logically possible that our understanding of others' mental states would be secretly mediated by angels or other extraterrestrials without whom humans couldn't understand each other. This, however, is not a serious candidate for explaining our knowledge of other minds. To see why is helpful in that this brings out the dependence of the justification of Wittgensteinian logical clarifications on their capacity to clarify the function of relevant expressions and to solve philosophical problems. Whilst extraterrestrials mediating communication is logically possible, appealing to this involves an equally problematic ontological postulation as the postulation of essentially private mental states. Wittgenstein's account, by contrast, doesn't involve any such postulations, but only appeals to the well-known fact that mental states are connected with a variety of non-linguistic and linguistic expressions whose significance the traditional picture of knowledge of mental states ignores. Arguably the recognition of the role of these external expressions as part of our linguistic practices then enables us to solve the problem of other minds. This can be connected with the point in Section 2 that the criterion of correctness for logical and philosophical clarifications is that they enable us to solve relevant logical, philosophical, or conceptual problems. Wittgenstein's positive account of the use of psychological language can be seen as an illustration of this.[36]

With regard to the generality of logical clarifications, it's noteworthy that if Wittgenstein's account of pain language were understood as an empirical claim, it would be illegitimate to extend it to expressions of other sensations without further empirical evidence to support this extension. However, such an extension is perfectly possible in the case of a logical model. (Consider how expressions of love, anger, and so on can burst out of one, similarly to expressions of pain.) Such extensions are justified on exactly the same grounds as Wittgenstein's account of pain language itself: they are justified insofar as they help to understand the function of relevant expressions and to resolve relevant philosophical problems. As these points about the justification and generality of logical models show, the logical role of Wittgenstein's natural history based logical models is distinct from the logical role of empirical assertions. The justification and generalization of grammatical statements and models differ from those of empirical assertions. Consequently, Wittgenstein's natural historical approach can be described as follows.

The origin or source of a clarificatory model or picture may be natural historical observations relating to human beings, as in the case of *Investigations* §244. Importantly, however, it's possible to base a logical model on natural historical considerations, without the model being subsequently used to make empirical assertions about natural history. The origin or source of clarificatory models or pictures doesn't in this sense fix their use and logical status, as if it were possible to only make empirical statements about

---

[36] By contrast, the traditional philosophical account of the knowledge of sensations is problematic in that it gives rise to a conflict between the actual use of language and the philosophical account of the same. This constitutes an anomaly, with the traditional account failing to 'add up'. It doesn't allow us to understand knowledge of others' sensations, suggesting that ascribing sensations to others, comforting those in pain, and so on are somehow suspect modes of behaviour that don't stand up to philosophical scrutiny (cf. RPP I §§548–549). This illustrates again how philosophical problems arise from logical unclarities and confusions that give rise to conflicts within one's use of language.

empirically given phenomena.[37] Accordingly, stipulated logical rules, actual and invented natural history, actual and invented language-games are all equally possible sources for logical models. In short, what matters for logical clarification isn't what inspired such a model or what considerations it was based on, but the use to which it's put. Natural historical models/pictures, just like any other Wittgensteinian clarificatory models, are all employed as objects of comparison in the sense explained in Section 2, not to make empirical statements about language use. Consequently, Wittgenstein's naturalism is distinctive in that, although it can take into account contingent empirical facts about humans and their environment, it isn't scientific in the sense of empirical scientific explanations and isn't empiricist in the sense of making empirical claims about language.[38]

Finally, the question might be raised of whether the later Wittgenstein's methods are formal. As is evident, they don't involve formalization in the sense of the translation of statements or theories into a formal logical language (by contrast, see Carnap 1947). However, if, following the *Tractatus*, we understand formality as a matter of strict focus on the use of expressions, rather than what the expressions speak about, so that in articulating logical/grammatical rules we don't draw on the content or meaning of expressions and appeal to an understanding of what they speak about, the answer is affirmative (cf. TLP 3.326–3.33; see Note 13). Wittgenstein's later grammatical investigations can thus be understood as formal in the sense that logic is formal in the *Tractatus*. The difference is just that Wittgenstein's later notion of use is much broader than that of the *Tractatus*, not narrowly focused on referring and true/false representation as the allegedly fundamental modes of language use.

As noted, one key motive for Wittgenstein's later approach is the gaps in Fregean–Russellian logic opened up by its focus on grammatical rather than logical form, contrary to Frege's and Russell's original aspiration to free logic from its focus on grammar. Through his focus on use, the later Wittgenstein, by contrast, is able to move beyond these limitations of Fregean–Russellian logic and start filling its gaps with the help of his novel methods.

---

[37] This applies the other way around too: Wittgensteinian logical models might in turn be employed as the basis of empirical investigations.

[38] Penelope Maddy gives an account of Wittgenstein's logical naturalism in terms of scientific naturalism. Problematically, she shows no awareness of how this runs contrary to what Wittgenstein says about the impossibility of explaining logical necessity in empirical terms. Instead, Maddy explains Wittgenstein's rejection of scientific explanations as a personal idiosyncrasy (see Maddy 2014 and Kuusela 2015 for a discussion).

4 Doing Justice to the Complexities of Language: Wittgenstein on Names

In this concluding section I discuss Wittgenstein's later account of different kinds of names, names being one traditionally important topic of discussion for logicians. In the *Tractatus* Wittgenstein recognized only two sensible modes of language use, referring and representing, the former being the function of names and the latter the function of true/false propositions.[39] The early Wittgenstein is roughly following Russell here; although their accounts have important differences, the two share a similar conception of names (PI §46). On this account, names in the proper logical sense are logically simple signs that refer to logically simple objects that are their meaning, whereby logical simplicity means that names contain no symbols as their parts, and can't be further analysed or defined. Characteristic of this account, then, is that it identifies the meaning of a name with its reference; if a logically simple name lacks reference, it's meaningless.[40] Accordingly, an important further part of this account is that names in colloquial language are mostly not of this kind. They are complex and can be analysed into simpler names in terms of Russellian definite descriptions, such as 'the author of *Waverley*', by means of which the reference or meaning of names is identified, as exemplified by 'Scott is the author of *Waverley*'. On the Russellian–Tractarian account, the names in colloquial language therefore are (typically) disguised descriptions.[41] Partly motivating this account of complex names is the observation that the names of colloquial language such as 'the king of France' may lack reference and yet sentences or propositions involving them, for example 'There's no king of France', appear meaningful. In order to explain their meaningfulness, it seems that complex names must be analysable in simpler terms (Russell 1918/2010, 80–2; Russell 1912/2001: 29–30, 32; TLP 3.203, 3.22, 3.26, 3.216, 3.3, 3.3411, 4.01, 4.0311, 4.06, 4.22; for discussion of Russellian names, see Strawson 1950/2010).

The later Wittgenstein rejects both the preceding accounts of simple and complex names. He rejects the account of simple names on the grounds that this

---

[39] Whilst Wittgenstein describes tautologies and contradictions as senseless, though part of the symbolism (TLP 4.46ff.), the *Tractatus*' sentences that serve the purpose of introducing the concepts and principles of Wittgenstein's notation are nonsense. They couldn't be stated in the correct logical language. See Section 1.

[40] Two differences are that Russell regards the objects which names refer to as something we are acquainted with in experience, including intuitions about logical objects; Wittgenstein leaves the former unspecified and denies that there are any logical objects, as explained in Section 1.

[41] Relatedly, Russell and Wittgenstein reject Fregean senses as a surface phenomenon that disappears on analysis (cf. Frege 1966b). That is, they reject the view that, at the level of logically proper names, there could be different modes of referring to the same object, for example the Morning Star and Evening Star, which both refer to the same heavenly body under a different guise.

isn't how names are used. Ultimately, to ensure that they have reference, Russellian simple names refer to whatever is given in immediate experience, performing a function similar to the indexicals 'this' and 'that' (cf. NB: 70). As Wittgenstein points out, however, although a name can be explained through ostensive definition by pointing to its bearer, 'this' or 'that' can't be explained in this way. This is illustrated by the contrast between 'This is Scott' and 'This is this', employed to give an ostensive definition to the presumed name. Whilst the former sentence is an unproblematic example of an explanation of 'Scott', the latter doesn't explain anything (PI §38; for Wittgenstein's examination of his earlier arguments for the postulation of simple names, see §§46ff.).

As for complex names, Wittgenstein rejects the view that the reference of a name is its meaning. This would imply that names without reference are meaningless, but it isn't true that a name loses its meaning if its reference ceases to exist (PI §39). Proper names of characters, such as 'Moses', or generic names of objects postulated by obsolete scientific theories, such as 'phlogiston', illustrate this. Whilst statements asserting or implying their existence are untrue insofar as nothing in reality corresponds to these names, it doesn't follow that they are meaningless, as exemplified by 'Combustion doesn't release phlogiston'. However, insofar as we regard meaning, with Wittgenstein, as determined by the use of a word, we can say that such names are meaningful insofar as they have a use. And although the meaning of a name can be explained with reference to its bearer, this is only one way to explain its meaning; this possibility of explanation doesn't require us to postulate a bearer for each meaningful name (PI §43). Rather, meaning is what an explanation of meaning explains. Such explanations, which explain the use of the word, can be given, for example, by means of an ostensive definition, by stating rules for use, or by providing examples in the case of generic names (PI §560; PG: 59–60).[42] What 'phlogiston' means, for example, can be explained in terms of relevant theories, which then puts us in a position to examine whether the name refers to anything.

Let's look more closely at what Wittgenstein says about different kinds of names, starting with proper names of individuals and thereafter common nouns.

4.1 Proper Names

Wittgenstein also rejects Russell's account that the meaning/reference of a name is identified in terms of a definite description. He discusses this in the *Investigations* where he uses as an example the proper name 'Moses', which could be given a variety of different definitions in terms of Russellian definite descriptions. Whilst the meaning of sentences involving 'Moses' varies

---

[42] See Kuusela 2008: chapter 4 for discussion of Wittgenstein's account of meaning as use.

depending on the definition, there's no particular privileged definition. Thus, Wittgenstein rejects Russell's view that a name is equivalent to some definite description. However, neither is there a clear limit to how much of what one understands by 'Moses' should be true or false in order for the sentence 'Moses existed' to be false. Consequently, the meaning of the name isn't definable as a conjunction of definite descriptions either, at least not in terms of any determinate conjunction. Rather, Wittgenstein asks, is it not the case that instead of the name having a 'fixed and unequivocally determined use' for me, I have a 'whole series of supports in readiness' so that I 'am ready to lean on one if another should be taken from under me' (PI §79)? Or as he explains with reference to another similar example, 'I use the name "N" without a fixed meaning' (PI §79). Lack of a fixed meaning doesn't impair the name's use, however. The use of 'Moses' can tolerate that not everything about the identity of Moses is determinate.

It's noteworthy that Wittgenstein's account of 'Moses' also allows for the possibility that nothing of what we think about Moses is true, whilst the name still retains a use, meaning, and reference. Indeed, this possibility seems typical of figures, such as Moses, of whom we aren't certain whether they are historical or mythological. It might be that nothing we believe about Moses is true, and this itself can mean a variety of things, as Wittgenstein notes. 'It may mean: the Israelites did not have a single leader when they came out of Egypt – or: their leader was not called Moses – or: there wasn't anyone who accomplished all that the Bible relates of Moses – or: ... ' (PI §79). Our explanations of the meaning of 'Moses' by means of descriptions might thus be mistaken in a variety of ways, including the possibility that everything we thought we knew about him was wrong. But it doesn't follow that the name wouldn't have meaning and couldn't have specific reference (see next paragraph). Wittgenstein's account of Moses thus differs from how Searle explains the notion of so-called cluster concepts, reminiscent of Wittgenstein's account of Moses in that cluster concepts allow that only some of the descriptions in terms of which their meaning would be explained and reference identified are true. A crucial difference here is Searle's requirement that some of those descriptions or explanations must be true in order for there to be a determinate reference for the name and a truth-value to corresponding sentences (Searle 1958: 170–1; cf. Kripke 1981: 31).[43] Arguably, however, this requirement is unnecessary and it gives rise to problems that can be avoided by dropping it.

---

[43] Searle formulates this as follows: 'To use a proper name referringly is to presuppose the truth of certain uniquely referring descriptive statements, but it isn't ordinarily to assert these statements or even to indicate which exactly are presupposed' (1958: 171).

With Wittgenstein, we can think that the use of a name might be passed on to users in such a way that the descriptions associated with it gradually became more and more fanciful about its actual bearer, until everything was enshrouded in falsity. Perhaps what is related about Moses was originally about a real person but then a development like this took place, with Moses himself adding many exaggerated falsities to the stories at an old age. We can thus imagine that the original Moses didn't do anything the Biblical Moses is claimed to have done, although a few similar things did happen. (For example, he lived in the Egyptian court, not as the adopted son of the Pharaoh's daughter, but as the son of the Pharaoh's chef.) Nevertheless, in such a case the name could still be understood as retaining its reference to the actual person Moses; it's of *him* that the stories aren't true. Whilst the descriptions associated with his name, then, are all false, the name still refers to him because of the continuity of its current use with its original referring use, which wasn't based on any descriptions, just as the names of persons usually aren't. As this illustrates, the truth of the proposition 'Moses existed' could be seen as depending on whether the person who was originally so called existed, even though any descriptions we could now give would be false and the original Moses couldn't be identified in their terms. Hence, there's no need to follow Searle in his account of cluster concepts. The referring function of names doesn't depend on any associated descriptions but on their use. In this regard it's important, as Searle himself observes, that names, unlike descriptions, don't specify the characteristics of the objects referred to. This is important for the use of names because it allows language users to speak about relevant objects without agreeing about all their relevant characteristics – or any characteristics, as we can now add (Searle 1958: 170–1).

More specifically, explaining reference as dependent on the use of the name instead of associated descriptions is important because it releases us from the following problems that arise for Searle's account. As Kripke has argued, Searle's view has the troublesome consequence that whatever is taken to be an identifying description of the reference will on this account describe a necessary property of it. This seems problematic in that surely anything that Moses did was contingent. Insofar as an account of names implies that something he did holds of him necessarily, merely because this is how we identify the reference of 'Moses', it says something false. Whatever might be necessary about Moses can't be regarded as a function of what we happen to know about him or whatever we treat as his identifying characteristics (cf. Kripke 1981: 66–7, 75). Likewise, if someone else had done what Moses did, that person wouldn't therefore be Moses (cf. Kripke 1981: 83–4). The application of a proper name to its bearer isn't dependent on the features or the alleged features of objects in this way (cf. Kripke 1981: 48–9). As the modal problem can be summed up, an account such as Searle's that makes the nature of the bearer of a name dependent on how we descriptively identify it ultimately portrays necessity as dependent on our contingent linguistic practices in a way that makes necessity itself contingent (cf. Note 29 on the difference between Wittgenstein's view and Carnapian conventionalism). Nevertheless, the preceding doesn't mean that the use of a name couldn't be explained in terms of descriptions and other explanations of use; evidently we do sometimes use descriptions to identify the bearer of a name, as exemplified by 'Paul is the bassist'. However, this has nothing to do with what is necessary or essential about the person.

Kripke rejects Searle's account of cluster concepts on the basis of similar arguments to the ones just sketched (which I have made use of). However, his positive account of names differs from Wittgenstein's, as I have outlined it.[44] Rather than appealing to use, Kripke suggests that, in order to explain the possibility of referring to an object independently of any descriptions, we need to postulate a causal link or a 'chain of communication' from a baptism, whereby the object first acquired its name, to the name's current applications (Kripke 1981: 90–3, 96). Partly owing to Kripke merely providing a 'picture' rather than a (proper) theory, it isn't clear what the commitments of his account of a chain of communication are (Kripke 1981: 93, 97). However, there seem to be certain points of difference between him and Wittgenstein worth noting.

Firstly, from Wittgenstein's point of view, no 'initial baptism' needs to be assumed to have taken place in order for a name to acquire a use. A name might gradually acquire a definite use that is then passed on. This seems to be all that is needed; there need not be any identifiable beginning for the use of a word, even in principle. If so, baptism is an unnecessary theoretical postulate. Secondly, on the Wittgensteinian account there's no need to postulate any intention to use a name in the same way as the person who passes it on, contrary to Kripke's view that such an intention would be a 'condition' for transmitting a name (Kripke 1981: 96). Instead, one might simply adopt the use. Indeed, the requirement seems false that an intention to use the name in the same way would be a condition for passing on names, as indicated by how children pick up new vocabulary, including proper names. No explicit intention to use the word in a certain way needs to be present. Indeed, if such an intention were required, it would bring into question the possibility of passing on names to young children. For, just as the linguistic repertoire of children at the age of five typically doesn't allow them to form the intention to solve algebraic equations, likewise

---

[44] For a critical discussion of Kripke's causal account that makes similar points, see also Evans 1973.

their repertoire at the age of two hardly allows them to form an intention to use a name in the same way as whoever taught them its use. Kripke's account of passing on names therefore seems over-intellectualized. Passing on names is a matter not merely of communication between those who can already use language, but also of teaching language. But in the latter case we can hardly expect any sophisticated intentions on part of the learners.[45] (If this is correct, Kripke's intention-requirement isn't only unnecessary but also suggests a questionable picture of what passing on names involves.) Note also that postulating a tacit intention in the case of young children risks making the use of 'intention' so loose that the word ceases to be able to do any work in cases where we might actually speak of an intention to use a word in a certain way (to mean or understand a word in a particular way). Thirdly, insofar as an intention to use a name according to a certain description is part of either Kripkean baptism or the adoption of a name, Kripke seems not to have managed to leave behind the account of reference as based on description, contrary to his aim (see Noonan 2013: 119). That is, insofar as the Kripkean intention to use a name in a certain way amounts to an intention to use it according to a certain description, such intentions risk smuggling back in a necessary link between reference and description. By contrast, the Wittgensteinian account in terms of the use of a word releases us from these descriptivist commitments as well as from the other mentioned complications relating to the notion of intention.

4.2 Common Nouns: Open Texture, Family-Resemblance, First–Third Person Asymmetries

What Wittgenstein says about Moses isn't intended as the basis of a general theory of names. Indeed, in the preceding section our focus was limited to proper names of individuals and it shouldn't be assumed that what holds for 'Moses' holds for common nouns. Wittgenstein remarks on names generally (in connection with his rejection of the Russellian logically simple names): 'we call *very different* things "names"; the word "name" serves to characterize many different, variously related, kinds of use of a word' (PI §38). If this is correct, trying to account for all names in the same terms runs the risk of misleading simplification. Accordingly, the last quotation can be read as recommending the adoption of an account of the concept of a name as a family-resemblance concept: names constitute a variously related set of uses of words. (For the

---

[45] I am ignoring the possibility of intentions formulated in a postulated language of thought à la Jerry Fodor or syntactical hypotheses in the style of Noam Chomsky, given Wittgenstein's rejection of relevant kinds of postulated linguistic structures. Whoever postulates Kripkean intentions at this level also has the burden of justifying the hypothesis regarding an innate mental language.

notion of family-resemblance, see below.) For example, whilst many types of names may share with 'Moses' the feature that their use isn't governed by definite rules, this negative characterization doesn't imply that their use would be otherwise similar to 'Moses'.

In the *Investigations* Wittgenstein immediately moves on from Moses to a different example of the use of a name, the common noun 'chair'. Here conceptual boundaries are blurred as in the case of Moses, but for a different reason: the rules for the use of the word don't cover its use overall but have gaps. Consequently, the truth-conditions for the use of the word are porous, failing to cover all possible cases of its employment, to use a term from Friedrich Waismann, Wittgenstein's collaborator in the 1930s. (Relatedly, Waismann describes this kind of concept as open-textured (1968).) To make his point, Wittgenstein imagines a chair that keeps disappearing and reappearing. Although such behaviour by a chair would create confusion about whether the object could be called a 'chair',[46] this possibility doesn't make 'chair' meaningless in general. The problem is contained in that the absence of rules for such peculiar occasions doesn't affect the use of the word in more usual contexts (PI §80). This can be connected with a point that Wittgenstein makes a little earlier in the *Investigations* (§68). Just as the absence of a rule for how high to throw a ball in tennis doesn't mean that the game isn't really regulated by rules or that it's unplayable, similarly the absence of rules for the disappearance and reappearance of chairs doesn't mean that 'chair' is meaningless or that the language-game with it is unplayable. In both cases, regularities of nature tend to take care of any problems with the gaps in the rules, making them practically irrelevant. (Tennis players don't need to be stopped from pitching the ball too high; chairs rarely disappear and reappear without explanation.)

Whilst the examples of a chair and Moses share the feature of having blurred borders, they are evidently quite different. Unlike with 'Moses', it isn't that we have 'a whole series of supports in readiness' for the use of 'chair', as if its meaning were not fixed. For most purposes it seems satisfactory to characterize a chair as a seat for one with a backrest; here we don't have the same kind of uncertainty and unclarity about the identity of the object that characterizes 'Moses'. Rather, the use of 'chair' is based on certain relatively simple criteria, on the basis of which we identify objects as chairs. However, this doesn't mean that language users would be able to come up with statements regarding those criteria or that they would identify chairs on the basis of any explicit lists of criterial features or descriptions. A good definition might not be easy to come

---

[46] When the chair first reappears after having disappeared, perhaps we will regard its disappearance as an illusion. By the fourth time, this explanation has lost its plausibility, however, and we are faced with the question of whether the word 'chair' is applicable to the object.

by, even in the case of such a familiar and simple object as a chair, and, as Wittgenstein points out, the ability to use language doesn't entail the ability to describe its uses, including the circumstances in which words are learned or applied to relevant objects (Z §§111, 114–116).

Now, to further illustrate the variety of names, another different kind of use of common nouns is their use to express what Wittgenstein calls 'family-resemblance concepts'. Characteristic of such concepts is that there's no common feature or common features that all cases falling under the concept share, and with reference to which the concept's extension could be defined. An example of a family-resemblance concept discussed by Wittgenstein is language. He writes about this, and his earlier account of language:

> Here we come up against the great question that lies behind all these considerations. – For someone might object against me: 'You make things easy for yourself! You talk about all sorts of language-games, but have nowhere said what is essential to a language-game, and so to language: what is common to all these activities, and what makes them into language or parts of language. So you let yourself off the very part of the investigation that once gave you yourself most headache, the part about the *general form of proposition* and of language.'
>
> And this is true. – Instead of pointing out something common to all that we call language, I'm saying that these phenomena have no one thing in common in virtue of which we use the same word for all, – but there are many different kinds of affinity between them. And on account of this affinity, or these affinities, we call them all 'languages'. (PI §65)

Contrary to what Wittgenstein assumed in the *Tractatus*, he now jettisons the assumption that cases falling under a concept, such as language, must share a common feature or features, and that this is the basis for applying the same word to them or for regarding relevant cases as falling under one and the same concept. As he notes in a remark from the 1930s, 'This conception is, in a certain sense, *too primitive*. What a concept-word indicates is certainly a kinship between objects, but this kinship need not be the sharing of a common property or a constituent' (MS 140: 31; cf. PG: 75). Rather, cases that belong to the extension of a family-resemblance concept are akin to one another in various ways, a point which Wittgenstein then seeks to explain in the *Investigations* with reference to the less controversial example of games (PI §§65–66). He concludes: 'And the upshot of these considerations is: we see a complicated network of similarities overlapping and criss-crossing: similarities in the large and in the small' (PI §66).

Similarly, Wittgenstein describes different kinds of numbers as constituting a family. Whilst some number kinds are called 'numbers' because of their direct relationship with what we have called 'number' until now, other number kinds are called by the same name because of their indirect relation to the more basic cases (PI §67; see below). But, Wittgenstein's interlocutor asks, wouldn't this mean that the concept of number is defined as the logical sum of number kinds? Wittgenstein responds: 'I can give the concept "number" rigid boundaries in this way, that is, use the word "number" for a rigidly bounded concept, but I can also use it so that the extension of the concept is not closed by a boundary' (PI §68). As he then goes on to argue by means of examples and analogous cases, this openness of boundaries doesn't mean that the use of either 'game' or 'number' wouldn't be regulated by any rules (PI §68). Neither is it the case that we don't really know what a game or a number is unless we define these notions (PI §70) or, *pace* Frege, that such a blurred concept isn't really a concept (PI §71). Whilst we can draw sharp boundaries to concepts, this isn't in general a condition for their adequacy or the possibility of their use (cf. Section 2.1 on idealization and abstraction). What is at stake isn't ignorance of conceptual boundaries but that such boundaries haven't been drawn (PI §69). Instead of being explained by means of definitions, family-resemblance concepts can be explained by means of examples that illustrate what sort of cases fall under the concept (PI §71).

Family-resemblance concepts can now be characterized as follows:

(1) The extension of a family-resemblance concept is determined by overlapping and criss-crossing similarities, kinships, or affinities, rather than by anything common to all cases falling into the extension (PI §§65–66; cf. §§67, 108). Thus, two instances might be connected directly by way of shared features or indirectly through cases with which the two instances share features without sharing any between themselves (PI §67; cf. MS 140: 32–33; PG: 75–76).

(2) Consequently, family-resemblance concepts have open rather than closed boundaries. New cases can be introduced into their extension without these cases having to share common features with all the old cases, and without their falling into the scope of a definition in terms of common features. Hence, new cases may extend the concept into new directions, adding new facets to the concept, and such additions can again constitute the basis for further extensions (PI §§68–69, 76).

The two characteristics of family-resemblance concepts, that is, direct and indirect connections between cases and relatedness through similarities or kinships, then define the mode of unity of family-resemblance concepts. On the one hand, the feature of there being direct and indirect connections between cases explains the openness of their boundaries. On the other hand, the feature of there being kinships or similarities between the cases distinguishes family-resemblance concepts from others, such as Moses, that likewise aren't used according to definite rules and that have no privileged definition, or whose use isn't overall bounded by rules, such as the concept of a chair. Evidently, the different possible definitions of 'Moses' don't have similarities between them on which the justification of treating Moses as a single concept would depend. No similarity exists between his being adopted by the daughter of a Pharaoh and his leading a people out of slavery or whatever else Moses did. Hence, although various connections may exist between the definitions of 'Moses' – for example, that he led his people out of slavery as their leader – Moses isn't a family-resemblance concept.[47] Still, the different definitions of 'Moses' are explanations of a single concept, like the different kinds of cases falling under a family-resemblance concept and the different uses of relevant words make up a single concept. As Wittgenstein remarks with reference to the concept of good more specifically, which he also regards as a family-resemblance concept, the different related uses of a family-resemblance concept can be regarded as different facets of a single concept (MS 140: 33; cf. PG: 77; quoted in Section 3.2).[48]

In the case of family-resemblance, the unity of the concept, and what belongs to its extension, therefore depend on criss-crossing similarities. This doesn't mean that whatever belongs in the extension of a concept is identified on the basis of descriptions of such features, or that the use of relevant words would be based on descriptions in this sense. As noted, the ability to use language and to describe its use are distinct and the former doesn't imply the latter. Accordingly, a typical way to explain a family-resemblance concept is by means of examples. Nevertheless, it's the similarities between them that justify the application of a name to the different instances of the family. Or, as Wittgenstein says, it's the kinships between the cases on the basis of which we apply a single concept to them (PI §65; MS 140: 32).

As regards other uses of common nouns, which we have by no means exhausted, it's no part of Wittgenstein's view that they should be expected to conform to either the model of open-textured concepts, like the chair, or that of family-resemblance. An important example of this, briefly discussed in Section 3, is psychological concepts. Typically, they involve a distinction and an asymmetry between first-person and third-person uses, as illustrated by the possibility of expressing or manifesting one's own pain, but not the pain of

---

[47] Strangely, Kripke reads Wittgenstein as claiming that Moses is a family-resemblance concept (1981: 33). This is strange because Wittgenstein clearly intends family-resemblance as an account of the unity of certain kinds of common nouns, characteristic of which is that different related cases fall into their extension, whilst Moses is the proper name of an individual.

[48] Whether Wittgenstein regards good as a family-resemblance concept is controversial but see Kuusela 2019b.

others, and of describing one's pain as well as making true/false knowledge claims about the pain of others (Z §472; PI §§244, 253, 293, 304). Here, too, it's natural to speak of different facets of use that constitute a single concept, even though this doesn't make pain a family-resemblance concept. Likewise it's crucial that the different facets of use constitute a single concept. As noted, a psychological state that I might express myself as being in – for example, that I am perceiving (seeing, hearing, smelling) something – must be the same state to which you can refer in the third person – for example, in order to ask me to confirm whether I perceive the same as you (cf. Note 33). The different facets thus have an essential unity that can't be broken without giving rise to anomalies in the account of psychological concepts.

4.3 Further Uses of Words

To conclude this discussion of names, Wittgenstein notes about the diversity of the uses of language that:

> There are *countless* kinds; countless different kinds of use of all the things we call 'signs', 'words', 'sentences'. And this diversity isn't something fixed, given once for all; but new types of language, new language-games, as we may say, come into existence and others become obsolete and get forgotten. (We can get a rough picture of this from the changes in mathematics.) (PI §23)

In this section we have barely scratched the surface. Not only are there established uses of words of the kind discussed in the preceding, and many other kinds too. Further, words with established uses can also be made new use of in what Wittgenstein calls a 'secondary sense'. This is exemplified by the expression or description (it could be either) of one's mental state by saying 'Everything seems unreal', where the primary use of 'unreal' has to do with whether something is real, not with mental states (RPP I §125). Another example is Wayne Shorter's instruction to the keyboardist Danilo Pérez to 'Put more water in those chords' (Mercer 2004: 256). Characteristic of such secondary uses is that, although the word can only be explained in the primary sense, knowledge of which is a precondition for understanding the secondary use, a novel employment is made of the word such that the interlocutor might either understand or fail to understand it (PPF §§274–278). Thus, Pérez, for example, had to spend the night pondering what Shorter had asked him to do. Upon his attempting to play as instructed the next day, Shorter approved, adding, 'But the water has to be clean' (Mercer 2004: 256).

As illustrated by the two examples, typical instances of secondary uses are expressions and descriptions of mental states and the uses of words in aesthetic contexts. However, they are also prevalent, for example, in philosophy, as when ascribing pain to inanimate objects, thereby disregarding the external manifest-ations of pain as playing any essential role in the application of the concept (PI §282). In such contexts it's then important to distinguish secondary from primary uses to avoid the risk of philosophical confusion. A secondary use might misleadingly give the impression of being part of the primary use, as when a philosopher declares the ascription of pains to inanimate objects a logical possibility, ignoring the role that external manifestations of mental states generally play in their ascription. If Wittgenstein is right, this is merely a secondary extension of our actual concept of pain, comparable to calling a tea party for dolls 'a tea party', even though no tea is served there. Although nothing is wrong with such secondary extensions, we ought to be wary of the potential for philosophical confusion that may arise in some cases.

As Wittgenstein also notes in the last quotation from the *Investigations*, the uses of language aren't fixed. They are dynamic and changing, an important example of the changing character of use being the hardening of contingent features of use into rules, whereby such features become an essential part of the use of the word (OC §§96–99). This is exemplified by the historical develop-ment in the course of which the chemical composition of water as H_2O, originally established as an empirical discovery, was turned into a defining, essential, or necessary characteristic of water, with water thereafter defined as H_2O. Here the use of the word changes, whilst also retaining the features of the original use and being continuous with it. (Such usages need not be entirely consistent. Even if we define water as H_2O, it isn't advisable to drink pure H_2O.)

Finally, as regards proper names, the recognition of the diversity of their uses might also help to deal with issues such as the uses of names in fiction. Whilst in contemporary analytic philosophy attempts have been made to explain differ-ences such as the truth of 'Sherlock Holmes is a detective' as opposed to 'Sherlock Holmes is a ballet dancer' on the basis of a general theory of names that requires a name to have a reference in order for propositions containing it to be true, Wittgenstein's account of names suggests a different approach. Instead of postulating a peculiar kind of entity as the reference of 'Sherlock Holmes', we might treat the use of names in stories and their use to talk about the real world as a related but different language-game. What we are dealing with would then be different kinds of employments of names that partly overlap and can be mixed, as exemplified by 'Conan Doyle created Sherlock Holmes who is a London-based detective', but which have distinct features. Whilst the truth of a proposition about reality depends on whether anything in reality corres-ponds to the names in it, a proposition about a fictional character can be regarded as true if the proposition corresponds to what the fiction says about the character. (Mixed cases may require disambiguation with regard to whether the fictional name is used to speak about something in the real world or in the fiction, as in 'Sherlock Holmes, the violin-playing detective, made Conan Doyle famous'.) Thus conceived, fictional use isn't reducible to, or explainable in terms of, the use of names to speak about the real world. Consequently, there's no need to postulate references for fictional names and to expand our ontological commitments in this way. (Technically sophisticated accounts have been developed along these lines.) It should be noted, however, that this is merely a sketch of how one might approach the problem of fictional names from a Wittgensteinian angle. I am not proposing the preceding even as an outline of a proper account.

References

Abbreviations for Wittgenstein's Published Works, Lectures, and Correspondence

References to Wittgenstein's *Nachlass* (BEE) are by manuscript and typescript number according to the von Wright catalogue.

AWL   *Wittgenstein's Lectures, Cambridge 1932–35*. Ed. A. Ambrose. Oxford: Basil Blackwell, 1979.

BB   *Preliminary Studies for the 'Philosophical Investigations' Generally Known as the Blue and Brown Books*. Oxford: Blackwell, 1958.

BEE   *Wittgenstein's* Nachlass*: The Bergen Electronic Edition*. Oxford: Oxford University Press, 2000.

BT   *The Big Typescript: TS 213*. Oxford: Blackwell, 2005.

CL   *Ludwig Wittgenstein: Cambridge Letters*. Oxford: Blackwell, 1997.

CV   *Culture and Value*. Oxford: Basil Blackwell, 1998.

LW I   *Last Writings in the Philosophy of Psychology, Vol. 1*. Oxford: Basil Blackwell, 1982.

NB   *Notebooks 1914–1916*. Oxford: Basil Blackwell, 1961.

OC   *On Certainty*. Oxford: Blackwell, 1993.

PG   *Philosophical Grammar*. Oxford: Blackwell, 1974.

PI   *Philosophical Investigations*. Oxford: Wiley, 2009.

PPF   *Philosophy of Psychology – A Fragment*. The second part of *Philosophical Investigations*. Oxford: Wiley, 2009.

RC   *Remarks on Colour*. Oxford: Blackwell, 1991.

RFM   *Remarks on the Foundations of Mathematics*. Oxford: Basil Blackwell, 1998.

RLF   'Some Remarks on Logical Form'. In *Philosophical Occasions 1912–1951*. Indianapolis, IN: Hackett, 1993, pp. 28–35.

RPP I   *Remarks on the Philosophy of Psychology, Vol. 1*. Oxford: Blackwell, 1980.

RPP II   *Remarks on the Philosophy of Psychology, Vol. 2*. Oxford: Blackwell, 1980.

TLP   *Tractatus Logico-Philosophicus*. Translated by C. K Ogden. London: Routledge & Kegan Paul, 1951. Translated by B. F. McGuinness and D. Pears. London: Routledge, 2004.

VW   with Waismann, Friedrich. *The Voices of Wittgenstein: The Vienna Circle, Ludwig Wittgenstein and Friedrich Waismann*. London: Routledge, 2003.

WVC *Wittgenstein and the Vienna Circle*. Oxford: Basil Blackwell, 1979.

Z *Zettel*. Oxford: Blackwell, 1967.

Secondary Sources

Anscombe, G. E. M. (1971). *Introduction to Wittgenstein's* Tractatus. South Bend, IN: St Augustine's Press.

Carnap, Rudolf (1947). *The Formalization of Logic*. Cambridge, MA: Harvard University Press.

Carnap, Rudolf (1959). 'The Elimination of Metaphysics through Logical Analysis of Language'. In A. Ayer, ed., *Logical Positivism*. New York: The Free Press, pp. 60–81.

Carnap, Rudolf (1963). 'Intellectual Autobiography'. In P. A. Schlipp, ed., *The Philosophy of Rudolf Carnap*. La Salle, IL: Open Court, pp. 1–84.

Carnap, Rudolf (1967). *The Logical Syntax of Language*. London: Routledge & Kegan Paul.

Carroll, Lewis (1895). 'What the Tortoise Said to Achilles', *Mind*, 4 (14): 278–80.

Conant, James and Bronzo, Silver (2017). 'The Resolute Readings of the *Tractatus*'. In H.-J. Glock and J. Hyman, eds., *A Companion to Wittgenstein*. Oxford: Blackwell, pp. 175–94.

Evans, Gareth (1973). 'The Causal Theory of Names'. *Proceedings of the Aristotelian Society*, Supplementary Volume 47: 187–208.

Frege, Gottlob (1966a). 'On Concept and Object'. In P. Geach and M. Black, eds., *Translations from the Philosophical Writings of Gottlob Frege*. Oxford: Basil Blackwell, pp. 42–55.

Frege, Gottlob (1966b). 'On Sense and Reference'. In P. Geach and M. Black, eds., *Translations from the Philosophical Writings of Gottlob Frege*. Oxford: Basil Blackwell, pp. 56–78.

Frege, Gottlob (1972a). *Conceptual Notation and Related Articles*. Ed. T. W. Bynum. Oxford: Clarendon Press.

Frege, Gottlob (1972b). 'On the Aim of the "Conceptual Notation"'. In T. W. Bynum, ed., *Conceptual Notation and Related Articles*. Oxford: Clarendon Press, pp. 90–100.

Frege, Gottlob (1972c). 'On the Scientific Justification of a Conceptual Notation'. In T. W. Bynum, ed., *Conceptual Notation and Related Articles*. Oxford: Clarendon Press, pp. 83–9.

Frege, Gottlob (1979). *Posthumous Writings*. Ed. H. Hermes, F. Kambartel, and F. Kaulbach. Oxford: Basil Blackwell.

Goldfarb, Warren (1997). 'Metaphysics and Nonsense: On Cora Diamond's *The Realistic Spirit*'. *Journal of Philosophical Research*, 22 (1): 57–73.

Grattan-Guinness, Ivor (2000). *The Search for Mathematical Roots 1870–1940: Logics, Set Theory and the Foundations of Mathematics from Cantor through Russell to Gödel*. Princeton, NJ: Princeton University Press.

Hacker, P. M. S. (1986). *Insight and Illusion*. Oxford: Clarendon Press.

Hacker, P. M. S. (1996). *Wittgenstein's Place in Twentieth-Century Analytic Philosophy*. Oxford: Blackwell.

Hacker, P. M. S. (2000). 'Was He Trying to Whistle It'. In A. Crary and R. Read, eds., *The New Wittgenstein*. London: Routledge, pp. 353–88.

Hanna, Robert (2006). *Rationality and Logic*. Cambridge, MA: MIT Press.

Hilmy, S. Stephen (1987). *The Later Wittgenstein: The Emergence of a New Philosophical Method*. Oxford: Blackwell.

Kripke, Saul (1981). *Naming and Necessity*. Oxford: Blackwell.

Kripke, Saul (1982). *Wittgenstein on Rules and Private Language*. Oxford: Blackwell.

Kuusela, Oskari (2008). *The Struggle against Dogmatism: Wittgenstein and the Concept of Philosophy*. Cambridge, MA: Harvard University Press.

Kuusela, Oskari (2011). 'The Development of Wittgenstein's Philosophy'. In O. Kuusela and M. McGinn, eds., *The Oxford Handbook of Wittgenstein*. Oxford: Oxford University Press, pp. 597–619.

Kuusela, Oskari (2015). 'Review of Penelope Maddy, The Logical Must'. *Nordic Wittgenstein Review*, 4 (1): 233–6.

Kuusela, Oskari (2016). 'Wittgenstein and Consciousness'. In S. Leach and J. Tartaglia, eds., *Consciousness and the Great Philosophers*. London: Routledge, pp. 199–208.

Kuusela, Oskari (2019a). 'On Wittgenstein's and Carnap's Conceptions of the Dissolution of Philosophical Problems, and against a Therapeutic Mix: How to Solve the Paradox of the *Tractatus*'. *Philosophical Investigations*, 42 (3): 213–40.

Kuusela, Oskari (2019b). 'Wittgenstein and the Unity of Good'. *European Journal of Philosophy*, 28 (2): 428–44.

Kuusela, O. (2019c). *Wittgenstein on Logic as the Method of Philosophy: Re-examining the Roots and Development of Analytic Philosophy*. Oxford: Oxford University Press.

Kuusela, Oskari (2019d). 'Wittgenstein's Reception of Socrates'. In C. Moore, ed., *Brill's Companion to the Reception of Socrates*. Leiden: Brill, pp. 883–907.

Kuusela, Oskari (2021). 'Wittgenstein's *Grundgedanke* as the Key to the *Tractatus*'. *Teorema*, 40 (2): 83–99.

Kuusela, Oskari (forthcoming). 'Wittgenstein's *Tractatus* without Paradox: Propositions as Pictures'. *Aurora Journal of Philosophy*.

Maddy, Penelope (2014). *The Logical Must: Wittgenstein on Logic*. Oxford: Oxford University Press.

McGinn, Marie (2006). *Elucidating the Tractatus*. Oxford: Oxford University Press.

Mercer, Michelle (2004). *Footprints: The Life and Work of Wayne Shorter*. New York: Tarcher/Penguin.

Noonan, Harold (2013). *Kripke and* Naming and Necessity. London: Routledge.

Read, Rupert and Deans, Rob (2003). 'Nothing is Shown: A "Resolute" Response to Mounce, Emiliani, Koethe and Vilhauer'. *Philosophical Investigations*, 26 (3): 239–68.

Read, Rupert and Deans, Rob (2011). 'The Possibility of a Resolutely Resolute Reading of the *Tractatus*'. In R. Read and M. Lavery, eds., *Beyond the Tractatus Wars*. London: Routledge, pp. 149–70.

Russell, Bertrand (1926). *Our Knowledge of the External World: As a Field for Scientific Method in Philosophy*. London: George Allen & Unwin.

Russell, Bertrand (1959). *My Philosophical Development*. London: George Allen & Unwin.

Russell, Bertrand (2001). *The Problems of Philosophy*. Oxford: Oxford University Press.

Russell, Bertrand (2010). *The Philosophy of Logical Atomism*. London: Routledge.

Searle, John (1958). 'Proper Names'. *Mind*, 67 (266): 166–73.

Strawson, Peter (2010). 'On Referring'. In *Logico-Linguistic Papers*. Aldershot: Ashgate, pp. 1–27.

Waismann, Friedrich (1968). 'Verifiability'. In R. Harré, ed., *How I See Philosophy*. London: Macmillan, pp. 39–66.

Acknowledgements

I'm grateful to the following colleagues, friends, and students for their comments: John Collins, Mauro Engelmann, Mirja Harkimo, Andrew Lugg, Marco Marchesin, Harry McMullan, Harry Rudman, and Mohamed Yillah. Likewise I'm grateful for feedback from the two anonymous reviewers for Cambridge University Press, and to the editor for the Elements in the Philosophy of Ludwig Wittgenstein series, David Stern.

Cambridge Elements ≡

The Philosophy of Ludwig Wittgenstein

David G. Stern

University of Iowa

David G. Stern is a Professor of Philosophy and a Collegiate Fellow in the College of Liberal Arts and Sciences at the University of Iowa. His research interests include history of analytic philosophy, philosophy of language, philosophy of mind, and philosophy of science. He is the author of *Wittgenstein's Philosophical Investigations: An Introduction* (Cambridge University Press, 2004) and *Wittgenstein on Mind and Language* (Oxford University Press, 1995), as well as more than 50 journal articles and book chapters. He is the editor of *Wittgenstein in the 1930s: Between the 'Tractatus' and the 'Investigations'* (Cambridge University Press, 2018) and is also a co-editor of the *Cambridge Companion to Wittgenstein* (Cambridge University Press, 2nd edition, 2018), *Wittgenstein: Lectures, Cambridge 1930–1933, from the Notes of G. E. Moore* (Cambridge University Press, 2016) and *Wittgenstein Reads Weininger* (Cambridge University Press, 2004).

About the Series

This series provides concise and structured introductions to all the central topics in the philosophy of Ludwig Wittgenstein. The Elements are written by distinguished senior scholars and bright junior scholars with relevant expertise, producing balanced and comprehensive coverage of the full range of Wittgenstein's thought.

Cambridge Elements ≡

The Philosophy of Ludwig Wittgenstein

Printed in the United States
by Baker & Taylor Publisher Services